ENERGIZE

IGNITE PASSION AND PERFORMANCE
WITH USER FRIENDLY
BRAIN TOOLS

Bob Faw

Energize: Ignite Passion and Performance with User Friendly Brain Tools

by Bob Faw

To purchase copies of Energize: Ignite Passion and Performance with User-Friendly Brain Tools in large quantities at wholesale prices, please contact Aloha Publishing at alohapublishing@gmail.com.

Cover design: Cari Campbell and Andy Harl
Interior Design: Andy Harl
Primary Editor: Stacy Ennis

Print ISBN: 978-1-61206-063-7
eBook ISBN: 978-1-61206-064-4
Library of Congress Control Number: 2013934788

Second Printing

Published by: AlohaPublishing.com

Printed in United States of America

"The problem, often not discovered until late in life, is that when you look for things in life like love, meaning, motivation, it implies they are sitting behind a tree or under a rock. The most successful people in life recognize, that in life they create their own love, they manufacture their own meaning, they generate their own motivation."

Neil deGrasse Tyson

DEDICATION

I dedicate this book to all of the individuals who have inspired me to dream beyond my horizon. I'm also indebted to those who have energized me to go after my dreams.

TABLE OF CONTENTS

INTRODUCTION

Countless centuries ago, three siblings were hiking back to their village at the end of a long hunt. The leader of the hunting party was named Thinker. Tall and brainy, Thinker was the planner. He was smart and analytical. The sister was named Artist. Thin, creative, and passionate, she loved making new things. Caveman was the most powerful. He loved the action of the hunt best.

On a hot, sauna-like afternoon, the siblings were trudging tiredly home after a long day of hunting. Artist was watching out for tasty fruit snacks. Caveman, on the other hand, was more worried about becoming a snack. He jumped at little noises and became irritable and argumentative at the slightest provocation.

Ignoring the others, Thinker thoughtfully stated, "I think I have a plan for surprising that woolly mammoth next time."

"What about the new net I made?" Artist excitedly interrupted. "It was so good! It almost brought the beast down!"

Caveman grumbled, "You dreamer! I was almost run over by that mammoth as it got outa your stinkin' net! It's good I'm fast and hit it with my club!"

"Quiet! I'm analyzing different options for our next hunt," Thinker replied.

Little did the three siblings know, just around the bend in the trail were two surprises. Tasty, ripe pears hung heavy on a tree on the left. On the right, a saber-toothed tiger hid in the bushes hunting for food for her own family.

Continuing to argue, they rounded the bend. Artist immediately spotted the pears and rushed for them eagerly. Thinker was caught up in his thoughts and didn't notice a thing. Caveman, scanning for danger as always, spotted suspicious movement in the brush. Instantly, he ran past Artist and scrambled hurriedly up the pear tree. Artist was still laughing at Caveman's frantic climb when the saber-toothed tiger pounced on her and then attacked the lost-in-thought Thinker.

For the purpose of explaining the way the human brain works I chose characters that represent three different aspects of how we think and feel. True cavemen (Cro-Magnon, etc.), of course, had all three aspects to varying degrees. Our distant ancestors with the more Caveman-type personalities were wired to constantly over-scan for danger; as a result, they were more likely to live long enough to pass on their genes. The Artists and Thinkers were necessary enough to survival that they passed on some of their genes too, but less so.

What does that mean to us? Many generations later, we have the genes of the survivors. We do have the traits of all of the siblings, but the strongest will always be Caveman's. We're children of countless ancestors who stayed alive by focusing more on threats than on the good stuff. We've developed what's called in science, a "negativity bias"; it's literally in our DNA to see the negatives in our lives as larger than they are and to minimize positives when we are scared. That works great in survival situations. Thank goodness for that tendency, but that same negativity bias gets us into trouble in social situations. It can also be a problem in everyday decision-making. In business settings, the Caveman part of us wants to resolve conflict by swinging a club or climbing a tree. We see this when people are blaming and running from responsibility in work relationships. We also see the Caveman's blame game in family life, whether it's nagging about chores, belittling the ones we love the most, or even becoming enemies.

However, blaming and focusing purely on negativity does not create solutions. It does not inspire people to go above and beyond. To be highly successful in the complex lives we live today, we need to rebalance ourselves by focusing far more on positives than negatives. We need to rebalance ourselves whenever the Caveman part of our brain wants to take over. It is more powerful than the Thinker and Artist combined. Otherwise we can be, what the mental health professionals correctly describe as, unbalanced.

Focusing on the positive activates the Thinker and Artist parts of our brains as well. When we're feeling down, it often takes great willpower to motivate ourselves to get a degree, try for a better job, or even be respectful to our loved ones. When the three characters work as a team inside of us, we do our best. We then have the emotional passion of the Caveman, the creativity of the Artist, and the logic of the Thinker. This "inner teamwork" can help us perform better in every area of our lives.

Even though we have all three of these parts of our brain, we tend to spend more of our time in one mode than the others. Personally, I tend towards the Artist. I love creating new ideas and sharing them with people. As a child, however, my Caveman took over a lot. I was defensive and lashed out at others. I've also had to purposefully develop my Thinker traits more as an adult to become more balanced. I trained myself to think more rationally by analyzing cause and effect rather than just going with gut feelings. Nowadays, I can get the three parts of my brain to work as a team most of the time.

You can probably think of people who tend to be more like one of the three siblings. In fact, you are probably inclined toward one of them as well. But it's important to use them all effectively to get what you want out of life.

I want to be really clear here. It's important, of course, to focus on threats and problems a certain percentage of the time. We'll always need the Caveman part of the brain to survive. However, in order to reach life dreams, we need to focus far more time on goals (Thinker), what works well for us and others, as well as new ideas (Artist). Spending too much time in Caveman mode tends to worsen relationships and reputations by angering others with our negativity.

By purposely focusing more on positives, we can give our brains a better balance of positive and negative thoughts and words. This enables us to make more balanced decisions by using all three

aspects of our brain. This also makes life easier and more enjoyable. Think about it: Optimists are more popular for a reason. We prefer people who see the best in us, rather than just our faults. Moderate pessimism is more helpful when fixing machines, making financial forecasts, ending relationships, and analyzing a process. Machines, money, and numbers do not have a Caveman and Artist inside. Optimism is more effective when motivating people, communicating ideas, teaching, performing athletically, starting relationships, and helping people persevere.

In this book I'll refer to "positive change" a lot. What I mean by this is a change process that yields positive results, and is also as positive to go through as possible. Of course there are plenty of necessary negatives to face in life, but there are many unnecessary negative experiences that can be avoided through using positive change tools. By learning the concepts taught in this book and putting the positive change principles into action, you will gain skills and a goal-focused perspective. This will help you to create a powerful and motivating balance for yourself and others. These skills can be used in every part of life to achieve more happiness, financial success, and better relationships. You can use them to create motivation, from the inside out.

I'm incredibly passionate about positive change and its power to energize people. The tools and ideas taught in each chapter have helped me transform my life, and they've helped many others as well. For the past twenty-five years, my days have been filled with sharing this passion. It's something I do daily through my work as Chief Energizing Officer at Matchbox Group and when speaking to leaders and organizations around the globe. My goal is for you to see the incredible power in positive change as it approaches, and intuitively understand how truly effective and simple it can be.

So, what do I mean by positive balance? It's more than just being happy or optimistic. It's the art of focusing more on your dreams. It's about thinking and talking more about what does work, and what to do, and spending less time focusing on what doesn't work, what not to do, or what to avoid. Even though it is critical to face hard truths, once we've done that, it's important to start creating more productive movement. A positive balance is key to igniting your own passion, as well as motivating others. Doing this well helps improve our performance and the performance of those we lead. This is true for your children, people you meet at work, a team you coach, or anyone else you need to influence to be effective.

What motivates me to keep teaching these positive change techniques to people and companies is that the principles can transform lives. I love seeing others improve their lives in small ways and in monumental, life changing ways. I also love helping leaders become more motivational, inspiring their organizations to increase passion and performance. It is so invigorating and meaningful to me that I have made it my life's work.

This positive change transformation has worked for me personally. It has changed everything about who I am as a person, friend, colleague, and even family member. People who attend my motivational and educational events are often surprised when they find out that I used to be a very negative person. I transformed the vicious cycles of a hard-knock childhood into the vital cycles of a rewarding adulthood.

You can relate if you've had the misfortune of experiencing violence, abuse, or neglect as a child, or even in your adult life. Having lived in some bad areas with gangs, race riots, and murder, my survival growing up was not guaranteed. At one of my lowest points, I was subjected to horrific violence and was very near death. Even inside my home, which was supposed to be a safe place, violence occurred, along with terrible confusion and guilt. These events led to depression, anxiety, and low self-esteem. Heartbreaking events like these affected the way I felt about myself at a deep level.

The internal chaos built up until, as a teen, my life spiraled out of control, and the world seemed only full of danger. It became easy to despise life, other people, and most of all, myself. There was so much emotional damage that living to the age of eighteen felt impossible. Life merely felt like a series of degrading events and low expectations.

Thankfully, even amidst the chaos, there were positive influences. As an older teenager, I had experiences that gave me a glimpse of how to make life better. There were occasionally wonderful people who cared enough to show a confused kid he deserved a better life.

One such experience began to shed some light on the power of influencing one's own "inner movie." My father hadn't always been able to protect me from the aggression of others, but he did try to help during some difficult times in my life. When I was seventeen, he sat down with me and showed me a book about depression. Even though I denied that it applied to me, I secretly read some of it after he left. Practicing one technique changed my life. The technique was to imagine a completely pure white wall and not think of anything else. Practicing visualizing that imaginary white wall quieted my anxiety and brought a rare feeling of almost-peace deep inside. This was a huge revelation. Up until this point, it had seemed impossible to positively influence my own mood (legally). The contrast of feeling more peaceful helped me recognize the constant state of anxiety that had been consuming my life. Knowing that it is possible to healthily change moods has been incredibly helpful ever since then. I learned how to identify what is actually happening inside, and what to do to improve it; and that knowledge has been incredibly empowering.

After turning eighteen—and, to my surprise, still being alive—it became easier and easier to connect with inspiring people. It was a powerful motivator to be seen as a good person! People seeing the strengths and goodness deep inside brought out more confidence and the courage to dream of a positive future. Some gave out unconditional love that was like water for a dying plant. All of these individuals gradually transformed my self-confidence and helped me dream for good things to happen in my life. Excitement for transformation began to grow more and more, and I began devouring books on positive thinking and influence. Positivity became the nectar of the gods!

I bet you, too, can look back and recognize those wonderful people and ideas that have helped you to create vital cycles in your life.

Having learned ways of gradually transforming, I have continually searched for new ways to transform that were easier, faster, and smoother. At the age of nineteen, I began to work with people in summer camps, after-school programs, and adventure trips. I realized I could apply the same principles and strategies I'd used in my own life to help others. My life's work had begun!

Since that day, I have eagerly learned more and more ways to energize positive change in myself and others. I read the latest in brain science research to help me understand why we do the beautiful and bizarre things we do, and based on that research, I've developed ways of motivating change.

In the last twenty-eight years, I've continued to learn, hone, and guide people with these tools. I've gained deep fulfillment helping others who have gone through major life challenges to transform their lives. In 2007, I co-founded a nonprofit called Vital Cycles with five others who have a similar passion for helping people turn their baggage into brilliance. Together, we've created Vital Cycles books and web resources, which are full of powerful tools for transforming the deeper, more "stuck" things that keep people from their dreams.

Today, I have a great life. I'm successful beyond my wildest teenage dreams. I travel the world sharing tools and ideas that can change lives. I make more money than I ever thought I could. I live in a beautiful house on a lake in New Hampshire. I have a sweet love and many great friends. And I, who once was so shy and depressed, now do motivational speaking on the concept of positive change in one's business and personal life! I make entertaining educational videos, write articles, and author books. I once hated my life; now I love it, and it gets better every year.

I want to share what I've learned to help you energize yourself and others. This book contains powerful tools for igniting passion for your goals, and inspiring the performance needed to achieve them. I've taught these to thousands of my clients and audiences over the last twenty-eight years. I have taken complex neuroscience discoveries and turned them into "usable brain science" that can help ignite passion and performance in your life and the lives of those around

you. And since the making of any good movie starts with the director yelling, "Lights! Camera! Action!" I'll use that idea to help define and explain the underlying concept of the book: the "inner movie." We start off with the "Lights!" chapters, which describe how people are motivated and become discouraged. The "Camera!" chapters then teach you how to focus your mind, thoughts, and words to energize for greater passion and performance. And finally, the "Action!" chapters guide you in developing your energizing skills.

Like anything else worth doing, positive change tools take practice, improvement, practice, improvement, and more practice. Life is short and precious! You deserve to make it as wonderful as possible.

PREPARE FOR IGNITION

Do you want to become great at motivating others? Would you like to learn how to ignite passion and performance in your life and the lives of those around you?

You can learn by reading, but building skill takes action. Since I want you to be as powerful at energizing as possible, this book is full of activities that are similar to the ones in my training programs. Next to each activity, you'll see this match icon, which represents an opportunity to "ignite" your skills through real life learning. Wherever possible, write down your answers, as that helps them stick in your memory.

I find that I'm also most likely to actually use the ideas if they're simple and I have all I need in one place. **To help you do that, download the free Ignite Workbook at ener-gizeperformance.com.** As you move through the activities in this book, find the section that corresponds with the activity you're doing and complete the writing prompt.

My hope is that you'll put this book into action to become even better at igniting passion and performance. In addition to the Ignite Workbook, I hope you'll find the free educational and entertaining videos available at matchboxgroup.com/inspiring-tools helpful. Equally important, I hope you will take the things you learn, together with the wisdom you develop, and share it with others to continue to help make this world a better place to live in. Together, we can be part of the positive change revolution.

CHAPTER 1

THE INNER MOVIE: COMING SOON TO A BRAIN NEAR YOU!

LIGHTS!
CAMERA!
ACTION!
SEE WHAT MOTIVATES
US - AND WHAT BRINGS
US DOWN.

Inner movies are stories that play in our heads and motivate us for good or bad results. They can impact our ability to succeed or fail at anything in our lives. The more we understand inner movies and learn to influence them, the more we can ignite passion and performance in ourselves and others.

Our inner movies replay memories of past events, things we wish we had and hadn't said. Most inner movies are created unconsciously, and often without our even realizing they're playing. However, we can create inner movies on purpose to help us achieve our goals. For example, while writing this book, I'm purposefully playing back memories of teaching about inner movies and what helped make the concept understandable to people. Inner movies can also help us plan for the future by creating images, ideas and motivating emotions about what we want to happen and how to get it to happen. For example, in my current inner movie I'm imagining someone reading this book, and I'm trying to anticipate what might be going on in that person's head as they read the words on the page rather than hearing me explain this concept in person. This inner movie motivates me to write more clearly.

We also use inner movies to anticipate possible successes or failures and imagine what we will feel like when we experience them. For example, I've also imagined what it will be like to hand out a copy of this book to all the people attending a speech I'm giving; this motivates me to write and design it in a way that really fits their needs. I've imagined that it will feel rewarding if it works and embarrassing if it doesn't.

In order to really "get" the concept of the inner movie, it's important to do the following activity. Fill out this table with your own personal answers. Most people have answers for around two of the four questions on each example; if that applies to you, just leave the others blank.

Take thirty seconds to think of each of the things in the left-hand column. Then, write your answers to the questions across the top row.

When you played an inner movie about each topic below, think of a:	What did you see in your mind?	What did you hear in your mind?	What emotions do you feel? (Did you feel happy, sad, regret, fear, etc.)	What other sensory stuff do you remember (scents, tension, spacy, etc.)?
Day dream that made you feel good.				
First day of school for you (any school).				
Time you were afraid of speaking to others.				
Funny thing that happened to you..				
Thing you really want to have in your life.				

As you thought about what to write in the chart above, your answers played in your inner movie. Everyone experiences inner movies differently. Some people see images in their minds; others hear the words being spoken. Some get more of an intuitive sense, and their inner movies are made up of feelings and emotions. Most of us experience a blend of these different senses. Notice what you experienced.

Here's a story to help you gain even more insight into how inner movies work and how they influence outcomes in our lives. Watch closely in a Motivational Leader story to see how team members' inner movies affect their moods—and their actions.

Maria "The Dynamo" Martin walked confidently into the meeting with Chin Wang, the new head of research and development. Maria looked far taller than her 5 feet 2 inches. The confident gleam in her eyes and perfect black hair made her look every bit the competent project leader she was. Chin grinned when he saw her. He had that predatory grin that told Maria there was a fun challenge coming up.

"What's up, boss?" she asked.

"Well," Chin replied, with excitement in his voice, "we've got the approval to make the Genius phone!"

Maria literally jumped in the air and pumped her fist. "Yes!" she shouted. "We're going to give Apple a run for their money! Hell, we're going to blow the iPhone out of the water!"

Chin grinned at her enthusiasm. An inner movie began to play in his mind of walking out on a stage in jeans and a turtleneck, telling the world about the greatest smart phone. No, he thought to himself, it's better than smart! It's a Genius phone! Watching Maria, he could see that she was just as motivated by the inner movie she was seeing in her head.

"Maria, you have one day to pick the top talent from anywhere in the company and create a top secret 'Genius Phone' team," Chin said. Maria's smile widened like the Cheshire Cat as she pictured herself telling the top talent what to do.

As Maria walked back to her office, she excitedly typed a text message to three people. She thumbed, "Drop everything. Get to my office at 4:00 today. Prep for big changes."

At 3:45, a heavyset, pretty blonde woman knocked on Maria's door. Maria called, "Come on in, Jenny. You're early."

Jenny's usually smiling face looked worried. "Is it layoffs? Did I take too many vacation days last month?" Maria looked at her, confused for a moment. The text had been vague, and Jenny's inner movie had formed an image of her out of a job.

Realizing this, Maria cried, "Oh! No, no, no, this is great news!" Jenny relaxed, and her smile gradually returned.

A dark-skinned, gray-haired man suddenly peered in the door with a concerned look on his face. "Everything okay here?" he asked. He continued grumpily, "Maria, you know I'm involved in several very important projects. How can you take me off of the Rocket project? I'm almost done with it."

Maria sighed. "I should have been more clear in my stupid text message! Sorry, Mech. You're the best hardware engineer in the company, maybe the world." Mech's frown smoothed out and his back straightened with pride. *"I figured you would give anything for the chance to be on the new Genius Phone team."*

At that, Mech rushed into the room excitedly. *"Well! Why didn't you say so, my dear? Let's get cracking. I see Jenny will be our marketing expert."* Jenny smiled and nodded. *"So, who's going to be on software? You know a holographic phone has never been attempted. We're going to need the best."*

They heard a cocky voice from the doorway, *"Yo, dudes. You're clearly talking about me!"* At 6 feet 2 inches (not including his spiky Mohawk), and weighing 140 pounds, Sly swaggered in. Jenny rolled her eyes at his cockiness. Sly continued, now looking angrily at Maria, *"You're sure getting bossy, ordering me to your office like that. I'm not some worker drone, you know."*

Maria shook her head in frustration. She realized that her poor communication has started off the best project she'd ever directed on the wrong foot. Soothingly, she said, *"Sly, soon you're going to be able to show Apple that you're the boss!"* That got Sly's attention, and he slouched over to a chair and sat down.

In this story, each person on Maria's new team had a completely different inner movie, which influenced different reactions to the same text message. Jenny's inner movie was of herself without a job. This caused her to be afraid. Mech's inner movie was of Maria pulling him from his other project because his work was not good enough, rather than to work on a better project. This caused him to be resentful. Sly's inner movie of being ordered around like a "lowly drone" influenced him to be angry and act arrogantly and rebelliously.

Maria, being the motivational leader she is, was able to energize each person's passion quickly. She soothed Jenny's fear by saying "great news" which helped her let go of the fear of losing her job. She inspired Mech with an apology, praise, and the idea of being on the best project. She calmed Sly with her voice and energized him with a vision of besting Apple. In later chapters, you will learn how to motivate people using these same skills, as well as how to identify and influence your own inner movies to create more passion for whatever you care about in life. Understanding how inner movies work—and how to use them—will also help you energize greater performance in yourself and others.

Activity 1:
Understanding Inner Movies

Think back over the Motivational Leader story and notice all the physical and emotional reactions that occurred based upon the characters' inner movies. Their inner movies changed from bad news to good news, even though the situation remained the same; it was just their perceptions that changed. This is true for all of us. Inner movies change our moods quickly and regularly.

Think about your day today and some of the inner movies you've had. Write the answers to Activity 1 in the Ignite Workbook (if you've downloaded it at energizeperformance.com).

The Brain: A Mental Simulator

Inner movies are constantly playing in our minds as our brains continuously try to make sense of what is happening around us. Sometimes we are aware of them, but more often, they simply play in the subconscious. They are our dreams when we sleep and our daydreams when we are awake. They are also playing with every thought and emotion we have. Sometimes they cause us to lose opportunities. Sometimes they help us break out of past ruts and reach for new experiences, take new risks, and think more positively about ourselves.

Inner movies are created by our brains from information gathered from all of our senses, blended together with memories of past experiences. Our brains are not able to actually see what's happening in the world with clarity. As Rick Hanson, author of *Meditations to Change Your Brain*, says, "The brain is like a mental simulator." Think of it like steering a submarine. You see what your instruments tell you, and you create an idea in your mind of what is actually happening in the ocean around you. But you rarely see the fish, other submarines, and boats directly. Our brains are so amazing at doing this, they make perception of the world around us seem seamless and smooth; it's like the most sophisticated virtual reality video game ever.

For example, when I was eighteen, I worked on a horse ranch that was also home to rattlesnakes. After my first encounter with a rattlesnake, I began to react as if every rattling noise was the tail of a snake. I'd even see a curved tree root and, in the first microsecond, think I saw a snake before I realized what it was. This simulator dynamic kept me alive, but anxious, in the canyons.

The bad news about the brain being a simulator is that it is easily fooled, even when it's not a survival issue. Here's a thought experiment for you: Think of a time when you believed someone was going to do something bad to you, only to find out that you were wrong about his or her intentions. That happened because your brain simulator played an inner movie of catastrophe and frightened the Caveman part of your brain.

For example, a colleague of mine once left me a voice mail saying, "Can you call me back? I'd like to give you some feedback about the retreat you ran." Until we talked three days later, my brain kept playing inner movies of bad things he might be feeling. Once on the phone with him, I was surprised to hear him simply say, "I learned so much during the retreat, Bob. It was a powerful lesson to me on dealing with change." I had wasted a lot of emotional energy preparing for negativity. That experience was a reminder that trying to guess in advance can backfire. If I can't stop the negative inner movies, I try to balance them out with inner movies of possible positive outcomes.

Inner Movies Fuel Motivation

Do you want to find out why some people are so motivational? Would you like to understand why, when you tell people to stop doing something, they usually continue to do it? Are you curious as to why some people go into a funk and can't seem to get out of it, while others seem to create opportunities and success everywhere they go? People's inner movies have a huge impact on all of these situations.

The bad news: Sometimes inner movies get stuck in regret mode— playing the "Woulda, Coulda, Shoulda" game. That is, thinking, "I would've done that, if only something different had happened!" or, "I could have done this if only someone did something right!" or, "I really should have done better!" This game tends to waste time and emotional energy.

The good news is that our inner movies can help us learn, prepare, and practice to be successful. The great news is that we can purposely influence our inner movies to be happier, more successful, and even better in bed. I'm only half joking with that last one, but using the inner movie well really can help in any area of life. In addition, it can help our relationships with other people and even help the way we feel about ourselves.

Side Benefits of Great Inner Movies

Since inner movies are stories that play in our heads and motivate us for good or bad results, it follows that high performers generally have very positive inner movies. Their inner movies help make them resilient, strong, and ready to deal with challenges. They know what energizes them and what brings them down. To ignite passion and performance, they work to keep up their physical and emotional health. They have inner movies playing that show them being healthy, strong and successful, which helps motivate them to eat well, stay active, and get enough sleep.

Medical research has shown that what plays in our minds—our inner movies—directly affects physical health. There is fascinating research showing that our thoughts affect stress levels, and more and more ailments that are now known to be caused by, or at least worsened by, stress. Stress has the negative side effect of preventing the immune (healing) system from kicking into gear.

On the plus side, inner movies can create a placebo effect and increase confidence that a pain medication can work. Just playing the inner movie of feeling more comfortable helps us to relax more, which allows the body to heal more quickly; and this is true of both physical and emotional ailments. When patients believe a medicine will work, they relax internally, which lowers stress (calms the Caveman). To play this kind of inner movie, visualize yourself feeling healthy, and think of all the nice things others do for you when you are sick. These kinds of positive inner movies both help relax you and allow the immune system to do its work better. This strategy isn't magic, and it won't cure things by itself, but it does help boost your immune system so that you heal faster when used with effective medical treatment.

Calming the Caveman in this way is essentially saying: By soothing the mind, stress (caused by the sympathetic nervous system) quiets down. This allows the immune system (activated by the parasympathetic nervous system) to help heal and relieve pain.

The Inner Movie: Coming Soon to a Brain Near You

Activity 2:
Side Benefits of
Great Inner Movies

Think of inner movies that play around your health. For example, "I never get sick," "I always get sick," or "I can't lose weight." Write about one that drags you down that you'd like to replace with one that helps you calm yourself and activate your immune system. For example, when I hear people around me sneezing, I tell myself, "I often stay healthy, while others are sick."

Each of us has an inner autobiography that has a profound impact on motivation, enjoyment of life, and even the ability to see ourselves as capable of a given challenge. We each also have a massive inner movie "library." It's like a chaotic scrapbook of everything that has had meaning to us in our lives. This library contains memories, experiences, and beliefs that are constantly producing new inner movies and adapting old ones. Behind all of these inner movie clips is the story we have about our lives, the world, and how we fit into it. I call this story the inner autobiography.

Inner autobiographies run our lives by telling us who we are and how we fit into the world. This is the brain's way of using past experiences to make us safe and successful in the present. It reminds us not to take bad risks that are similar to ones that have burned us in the past. It also reminds us of the best ways we're likely to get what we want. By the way, these lessons from the past sometimes no longer work for us in our lives today. We may need new inner movies to be successful in new situations.

Over time, everything we experience shapes our worldview. The more emotional an experience is, the more it impacts our inner autobiographies.

Starting in childhood, and progressing throughout life, we tend to see ourselves in a particular type of role, or character. Some of us see ourselves as heroes in our inner autobiographies. Some of us see ourselves as victims. A few even see ourselves as villains. This includes the concepts of self-esteem, self-worth, and even self-confidence, and our inner autobiographies define and limit the choices we think we have.

University of Illinois researcher Bonnie Benard looked through tons of research to discover what it is that helps children in tough situations become resilient adults. She found that at-risk children could often succeed if they had relationships with caring adults who had high expectations of them. I have experienced this firsthand. These wonderful, caring adults help create inner autobiographies of self-worth and potential for success in children. These positive autobiographies help children later in life by creating inner movies of confidence, and this confidence enables kids to see opportunities for success where their less fortunate peers just see another chance at failure.

Activity 3: Your Inner Autobiography

List some things that you notice about your own inner autobiography. Make sure to include some things that energize you for success, as well as some things that bring you down.

CHAPTER 2
THE A.C.T. TEAM:
THE ARTIST, CAVEMAN AND THINKER

What would it do for your life if you could be twice as motivational for yourself and others? We'll start with more brain science behind motivation. Our motivation level goes way up or down depending on which aspects of our brains are activated. Many find the actual names of parts of the brain hard to remember and confusing. I'll explain some of the brain science of motivation in usable and fun terms. Imagine that we each have an A.C.T. team in our heads. The team is made up of three characters: the Artist, Caveman, and Thinker (see the Introduction for the background story). These are the parts of our brain that motivate us, give us energy, and help us think intelligently.

When the A.C.T. team works well together, we have creative energy to perform at our best. It's important to know that the inner movie has a profound effect on these parts of our brain and how well they interact with each other. Here's how it all works. As you might recall, inner movies are stories that play in our heads that motivate us for good or bad results. These three brain characters react to what plays in our inner movies. Their reactions affect our brain chemistry. That brain chemistry affects our motivation. Our motivation (or lack thereof) is what causes us to act in a way that can get us those good or bad results.

For those interested in the brain science of it all: The Thinker is the prefrontal cortex part of our brain. The Caveman is the limbic system. The Artist is really a frame of mind that occurs when we are in the mental state of "Flow." Flow, as the psychology professor Mihály Csíkszentmihályi describes, is the mental state in which a person performing an activity is fully immersed in a feeling of energized focus, full involvement, and enjoyment in the process of the activity. To keep the concept of the inner movie simple and more enjoyable, we'll simply use the characters to describe how to use what we know about the brain for motivation and positive change.

Self-awareness is one of the most precious keys to self-motivation and to motivating others. Gain as much self-awareness as you can by understanding how our brains are influenced by words and tone of voice, and where you find yourself being motivational or bringing people down. I've worked on motivating myself and others for decades, and I continue to deepen my self-awareness all the time. It's critical for motivational mastery.

The Caveman

Power. Energy. Speed. Survival! We need these to accomplish our life goals.

The Caveman—or Cavewoman, if you prefer—is the most powerful part of the brain and represents the survival instinct, which is always searching for threats. (It's also searching for food and mating opportunities, but that's a topic for another book.) The Caveman is also the most primitive part of the brain. Its overwhelming focus on survival is a huge deal, and those survival instincts can overpower any other thought or desire. Obviously, we have to be alive to do what we like to do, so survival always trumps anything else. Even if the Caveman incorrectly perceives a threat, its reactions can be overwhelming. The good and the bad news is that the Caveman is very focused on negatives to protect us. It keeps us alive, but it also often reacts negatively when a positive approach would work better. More bad news: The Caveman is very rigid, reactive, irrational, and can take over in the blink of an eye. We all know someone like this— and we all have this quality inside us, too.

When the Caveman thinks it sees a threat, it triggers one of the "F responses": fight, flight, or freeze.

In the **fight response**, cortisol and adrenaline are pumped into the body to help focus on the threat, ignore everything else, and aggressively do whatever it takes to overcome the danger.

In the **flight response**, these same biochemicals give us the energy needed to make an escape.

In the **freeze response**, the mind becomes overwhelmed and causes the body to stop moving, and often stop thinking, in an attempt to not be noticed by whatever we feel threatened by.

Caveman's Confusion

While the Caveman is necessary for survival, it creates a lot of challenges for us. Because of the way the brain has to simulate reality, the Caveman cannot tell the difference between what's happening in reality and what's playing in an inner movie. This is a big, hairy challenge. Earlier, I told you about my brain perceiving rattlesnakes, even when they weren't there. This is the Caveman's way of quickly jumping to conclusions before it sees what is really happening. Here's how it works: Looking for proof takes too much time, so the Caveman must take over within milliseconds if it thinks there is a threat. It is constantly scanning both your inner movie and outside activity to see if anything creates a threat warning. So, even misunderstood, but not real threats trigger the Caveman into action.

For example, think of Jenny in the Motivational Leader story. A simple text message caused her to fear losing her job. Her Caveman reaction influenced an inner movie of herself without a job, and she ended up feeling really anxious. Maria had to reassure her and help create an exciting inner movie by telling Jenny about the great news.

I've had reactions like Jenny's many times. Think about a time you've gotten defensive, even when that very defensiveness made it harder to get what you wanted. By the way, if you're thinking, "Bob, I don't have times like that," it's your Caveman talking.

Another compelling example of the Caveman's confusion is illustrated in a Gallup poll about the top fears in America. This performance management research company discovered that, oddly enough, the number one fear in America is public speaking! Think about it. How many people do you know who have died from public speaking? Or even broken a limb? Or caught the plague? It doesn't happen. Even weirder, death is number eight on the list! Wild, eh?

Here's why: The Caveman part of the brain is so affected by thoughts and images of saying the wrong thing, being laughed at, or failing, among other things, that it sometimes goes into freeze mode. It's our brain's way of protecting us from what it perceives could lead to death. You know the expression, "scared to death"? That is our Caveman talking. Unfortunately, hearing the Caveman speak in our minds can make it hard to speak to others.

It's important to remember that all of the "F responses" are critical to survival and can be very helpful in some situations. Fight gives us the energy to protect ourselves when others attack us unfairly. Flight can give us the quick, adrenaline-fueled ability to escape an approaching saber-tooth tiger, out of control car, or other danger. Freeze can shut our reactions down when fighting or fleeing a threat may actually cause more damage than help. Think of the "deer in the headlights" look that a person can get when being yelled at by a boss or bully. (Too often, these two people—boss and bully—are the same when the boss lets a Caveman's fight response run the show.)

Daniel Goleman, author of *Emotional Intelligence*, calls "F responses" the "amygdala hijack" because the amygdala is the part of the brain that initiates fight, flight, or freeze. During fight or flight responses, the biochemicals adrenaline and cortisol are released. Adrenaline provides us with tons of energy—and fast! It helps us move quickly and push beyond our normal limits. Cortisol narrows our focus on the perceived threat. The great news is that this helps us respond well to real threats. The bad news is that when the threat is not real, these biochemicals push us to go too far and in a narrow-minded way. Even worse, when we go through long periods of stress, these biochemicals wear us down. Cortisol has been nicknamed the "stress hormone" because of its role in the creation of stress; it's a lifesaver, but too much of this good thing can become life-threatening. There are many physical and emotional challenges that are caused or worsened by chronic stress. Learning to identify when too much stress is happening (the "F responses"), and what to do about it, are necessary for being able to motivate yourself to a higher level.

Following are some examples of "F responses" that get us into trouble. Each one is directly triggered by what plays on our inner movies.

Fight

- **Attacking others.** This one is the most obvious. The more the Caveman's "F response" is triggered by a negative inner movie, the more we will attack even when it hurts our own goals. For example, sometimes I've noticed that I've nagged—yep, nagging is a fight response!—a family member to clean up. I've done this even though it doesn't work, and even worse—erodes our relationship. Having happy family relationships means a lot to me, and yet, if I'm not careful my Caveman can drive me to damage these precious relationships for a far less important thing like my standard of cleanliness.

- **Arguing, defending, or debating irrationally.** One thing I've noticed is that the more people are sure they're right, the more wrong they appear to others. In their inner movies, it seems completely obvious that they're right, and they feel a certainty that if they argue loud and long enough, others will see that, too. I've even seen a client threatened with losing his job continue to tell everyone they were wrong up until he was fired. It can be a vicious cycle. Other people's inner movies, meanwhile, see those people as arrogant, irrational, and not team players. I ask my clients who get stuck in this type of fight response, "Would you rather be right or successful?" Instead of always proving other people wrong, finding a common goal and working together are far more likely to lead to success. But try telling that to people when their Caveman is running the show!

Activity 4:
Recognize Your Fight Response

Write a few examples of when you've had fight responses. What did your body feel like? What emotions did you have? It's helpful to know how to recognize when you start to do this so that you can calm your Caveman and refocus on what's really important.

- **Blaming.** This one is huge! Have you noticed that the more strongly people blame others, the more they exaggerate, are blind to positives, and even outright lie? And I'm not just talking about politics, either. When we blame others, our inner movies get more and more exaggerated and distorted, and we see ourselves purely as innocent bystanders. Yet others see us as narrow-minded aggressors. The blame game is one of the biggest productivity drains at work, as well. You know the Caveman is involved when a person over-simpli-

The A.C.T. Team: The Artist, Caveman, and Thinker

fies a complex problem just to blame or attack someone. They stop looking for solutions and waste time, energy, and goodwill attacking others. Blaming is a common technique for motivation that almost always backfires at some point. It's a dead-end tool that creates vicious cycles. Instead, focus on building motivation techniques that help build momentum over time, creating vital cycles of good results.

Activity 5:
Recognize Your Flight Response

Write a few examples of when you've had flight responses. What did your body feel like? What emotions did you feel? It's helpful to be aware of these responses so that you can face your challenges and come up with solutions.

Flight

- **Avoiding conflict.** This happens in so many ways. Flight includes screening calls in order to avoid talking to someone we find threatening. Some people call in sick to get out of meetings. Have you ever found yourself walking down the hall, saw someone coming towards you that you didn't want to see, and quickly changed directions to avoid running into them? That's a flight response. Inner movies of anticipated frustration, pain, boredom, or fear cause these flight responses to dramatically influence thoughts, actions, and even tone of voice.

- **Procrastination.** I do this with paperwork I don't enjoy, such as taxes and proposals. Think about what chores, tasks, or interactions you tend to put off because you don't like dealing with them. In my inner movie, I see taxes as grueling mind-numbing work, and its doubly painful because I feel stupid so many times while doing them. This inner movie of expecting misery kicks off my flight response and causes me to focus on the pleasure of something I'd much rather do at the moment (like watch a movie).

Freeze

This is the dreaded "deer in the headlights" moment. The most common examples of this are stage fright, forgetting what you wanted to say, or literally freezing in place. This is caused by our inner movie playing images of failure, humiliation, and rejection. A person also may go blank when confronted by a very intimidating

The A.C.T. Team: The Artist, Caveman, and Thinker

person. You know you were in this situation when you later say things to yourself like, "I can't believe I couldn't think of what to say! I wish I had told him off! I wish I could have knocked them silly!"

Activity 6: Recognize Your Freeze Response

Write a few examples of when you've had freeze responses. What did your body feel like? What emotions did you feel? This one may be harder to answer. The freeze response can feel like your head is cloudy, it can be hard to hear people, and, in extreme freeze situations, you may not remember the moment at all. I sometimes freeze when I feel overwhelmed by numbers (complex math, taxes, or balance sheets). I can also start to freeze up when I'm expecting rejection.

The Artist

The Artist is an amazing dynamic in the brain and another key to igniting passion and performance. Being able to activate the Artist in yourself and others is a powerful motivational skill.

The Artist is activated when we have a good balance of the passion of the Caveman and the creative focus of the Thinker. The Artist fuels our passion for things we care deeply about. It energizes us to go to great lengths to build or protect these things. Your Artist is active when you are excited about a hobby, engrossed in a movie or enthralled by a performance. It's most active when you are enjoyably creating something. People in their Artist mode include: a gardener getting all sweaty and dirty but smiling about it; a computer programmer volunteering to help write Linux code for free; an expert adding information to Wikipedia purely for the love of sharing knowledge; a sales executive sincerely and passionately telling people why he loves the product he sells; an engineer excitedly finding better ways to make a process better; a scientist making a break-through discovery after years of dedicated research; and a child pretending to serve tea. Think of the things you most enjoy creating, writing, building, cooking, sharing, selling, describing, or doing. Chances are that your Artist is active and leading the charge. For me, public speaking, teaching, and humor are where my Artist comes out the most. I really do love the helping others to learn, grow, and have fun. This is where I feel the most alive, dynamic, and engaged with life.

Just as calming the Caveman is necessary to be productive, it's just as important to energize the Artist. This brain dynamic creates the excitement that motivates action. Similarly, when we motivate others, both the Caveman and the Artist are critical to successful change. Their energy can help make motivation work well. On the other hand, if the Caveman gets scared or angry, you've got another thing coming. In chapter one, Maria ignited the passion of her team by activating the Artist. She did so by using words, and an excited tone of voice, to create an energizing inner movie for her colleagues.

Using your Artist effectively is also key in accomplishing what you want out of life. For example, if you want to have a successful career, it's far easier to become great at something you enjoy doing. Choose work you find interesting, exciting, and that you can get passionate about. This taps into the power of the Artist. Look for ways to increase the amount of time you spend in the Artist mode (it can't be all Artist time, of course). Think about what you love to do and how much time you can easily spend doing that activity, even if plenty of other people would have to force themselves to do it. That's because everyone's Artist is completely unique, depending on genetic nature, and the experiences a person has had.

My consulting firm has developed a model called Best DNA to help people identify where their Artists can help them be more successful in their careers. Best DNA is the combination of what you love to do, are good at doing, and others will pay for. We have free videos and guides at matchboxgroup.com/inspiring-tools.

Activity 7:
Getting to Know Your Artist

Write about some of the activities that you enjoy simply because of a creative aspect of some sort. Also, write down some things others say or do that helps get this Artist energy revved up for you.

The Thinker

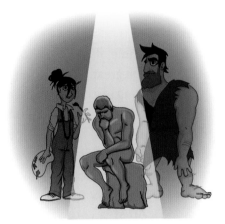

Here is more great news! The Thinker is another part of your brain that can help you succeed by thinking logically to help balance the emotions of the Caveman and guide the passion of the Artist. The Thinker can inhibit the Caveman when it wants to blurt out negatives at people. It is a part of the brain that is able to think more clearly, consider the future, and process big, complex thoughts. Most importantly, the Thinker is able to think about the consequences of our actions, which really saves your bacon. It helps you to pay bills, plan projects, create strategic plans for your business, use logic to find better solutions, study for exams, and write contracts, among many other things. The Thinker also helps you come up with ways to change your inner movies to be more positive and motivating.

Activity 8:
Getting to Know Your Thinker.

Write down areas of your life where your Thinker is a huge help to you. This brings the Thinker to life for you. It also creates inner movies that help the Caveman to appreciate the value of these tasks. For example, when I think about how doing my own taxes helps me to get a better handle on my finances, and my plan to save for retirement, I feel more motivated to get started on my taxes.

The Thinker lives in the front of the brain, the area called the neocortex, or as Daniel Goleman calls it, the "thinking brain." This is the most advanced part of the brain. It is a lot slower than the Caveman, so the Thinker often regrets what the Caveman blurts out when talking with clients, colleagues, or family members. The Caveman is fast for survival, and the Thinker has to put a lot more information together before responding. The Caveman wants to click "send" on an angry email. The Thinker hits "delete" and rewrites the email once emotions have cooled down. This is because the Thinker is aware of long-term consequences and how important good relationships are to success. It's also the part of the brain that keeps track of timelines, commitments, goals, and plans. We may need the Caveman to keep us alive and moving, and the Artist to give us the emotional energy to work hard and create new things, but we need the Thinker to help us make the big plans and to remember to get the little, boring details done as well.

Think about the three parts of the brain in terms of training and education. The Thinker gets you into the classroom and helps you learn the details and information taught. The Artist helps you dive into learning about topics you enjoy. And the Caveman provides enough fear of looking bad to get you to work harder for a good grade.

At work, the Thinker and Artist work as a team. Together, they help set goals, generate the passion to work for those goals, and plan next steps. The Thinker is the part of the brain that is taking the ideas from this book and thinking of ways to create inner movies that will energize your Artist. The more you understand about your inner movies and the reactions that your Artist and Thinker have to them, the more you can learn to be the director of your inner movies—and positively influence other people's inner movies, as well.

CHAPTER 3
INNER MOVIES RUN OUR LIVES—FOR BETTER OR WORSE

It's no exaggeration—inner movies really do run our lives! Even without the brain science, golf great Jack Nicklaus understood this fact, and he knew how to create a winning inner movie. He writes in his book, *Golf My Way*, "What we tell ourselves causes the whole body to respond to what the mind imagines is possible." What we think, what we believe, and what we see in our minds guides our actions. Inner movies are the stories playing in our heads that have been influencing our emotions, thoughts and actions our entire lives.

By really grasping the concept of the inner movie, you can gain a deeper understanding of how to influence yourself and other people. Often, you're not even aware of what is happening in your mind. But the more you learn about inner movies, the more you can energize yourself, rather than bring yourself down with old, outdated inner movies.

Positive inner movies motivate us to take important risks we need to take. For example, an inner movie in which you see yourself as competent can help in applying for a new job. Inner movies lead us to do many things that are good for us. For example, you might choose to pursue hobbies that you really enjoy because your inner movie plays past experiences of enjoying them. Inner movies help us to enjoy life greatly. There is an interesting piece of research showing that people feel happier anticipating a great vacation than while on that vacation! This is an excellent example of being so influenced by an inner movie that a person feels some of the pleasure of getting away, before even leaving.

Unfortunately, negative inner movies can also hold us back from doing things that would be good for us. An inner movie that continues to show potential rejection can prevent a person from applying for a job. People suffer a great deal of anguish and fear from inner movies that star themselves in situations where they are being ridiculed, hated, judged, slandered, and all of the other things the Caveman is terrified of. Even though most of these fears never come to pass, the damage has been done, purely from the inner movie. Mark Twain said it best: "I have been through some terrible things in my life, some of which actually happened." William Shakespeare said it more pointedly: "Cowards die many times before their deaths. The valiant never taste of death but once."

I do want to be clear here. There are times when a negative inner movie playing out a predicted disaster can also motivate us to be better prepared. Here's an example: As I was preparing to speak to 140 telesales reps at Monster.com on the topic of "Language of Influence," one inner movie kept causing me anxiety. I kept imagining the audience losing attention as I spoke and beginning to play with their cell phones. Thankfully, instead of freezing up, my Thinker stepped in, and I begin to brainstorm solutions to that concern.

The Artist part of my brain came up with some very creative ways to keep people engaged. I then felt more confident about my speech, and my inner movies were much more positive as a result. This helped me prepare well for this event. I was able to benefit from a negative inner movie because it focused my attention on a potential problem. Then, I had to create a positive inner movie with enough confidence to go on to solve that problem. If you find yourself facing a similar situation, use the negative inner movies to help you, but don't let them rule you. Recognize when to solve something and when to simply refocus on a positive inner movie.

Activity 9: Understanding Your Inner Movie

Write down a few inner movies that helped you in your life. Then, write about a few inner movies that have gotten in the way of your success.

The Hidden Power of Inner Autobiographies

Our inner autobiography is the background of our inner movie. It is our deepest sense of self. It runs our lives by telling us who we are, and how we fit in the world. To demonstrate how our inner autobiographies are formed, let's join Sally in her Teenage Angst story.

"Sally, Jasmine, Britney!" Sally's mother called. "Come on girls, it's time to go to church." The three sisters came running down the stairs. Sally, the oldest of the three, was carrying Britney's shoes. Her mother glanced

at them and directed, "Sally, be a sweetheart and get Jasmine and Britney ready to go." Sally dutifully helped them put on their sweaters and shoes, even though her own hair was a mess.

"Mom," Sally asked, "can we stop at the store and buy a new brush for me on the way to church?"

Her mother frowned, "Now, now, Sally, be nice. It's more important to be early and help set up Sunday school than to fuss with your hair. Don't be vain." Sally nodded her head meekly as her mother smiled approvingly and turned to go.

Later that week, Sally walked down the hall of her high school, trying to be small. Even then, she heard some of the cheerleaders making fun of her bushy hair.

When she told her best friend Cecile about their hurtful words later, Cecile warmly replied, "Don't worry, Sally, they may look good, but you are good! You're the sweetest girl in school. You help everybody out when they need it."

Sally lifted her head and squared her shoulders. "You're right! That's what's important." Then, she hung her head low again and murmured, "I just wish Billy thought that!"

Cecile smiled kindly and said, "Well, since he's the most popular boy in school, and the quarterback, every girl wants him to like her. But I don't even think he knows we exist. But at least John in English class likes you. He told me you're the friendliest person he's ever met."

Sally sadly replied, "I'm glad that people like me. I just wish I didn't always lose to the cheerleaders."

In Sally's inner autobiography, she is "nice but not pretty." She sees herself as "sweet and friendly," and that's a good thing! It was, after all, what people liked best about her. Her view of the world is that it's best to settle for being liked as a friend, and trying to be attractive to boys is a waste of time. She just assumes that the pretty girls would get the boys, and she will date whoever can't find a pretty girl to date. Sally believes that she can enjoy life overall, as long as she doesn't expect too much.

Our inner autobiographies have been transforming us all of our lives, even if we don't realize it. They run our lives by telling us who we are and how we fit into the world. Over time, everything we experience shapes our inner autobiographies. Family, friends, and media have constantly influenced our inner autobiographies. Books we've read, movies we've watched—all the ways we take in information shape us. The more emotional a situation, the more lasting an effect it has. Our own thoughts have the most impact of all. Inner autobiographies are much harder to change than fleeting inner movies, but the change is so worth it.

I want to clarify. When we "rewrite" our inner autobiographies, we're changing the way we interpret the stories about what has happened in our lives. We can't change the past, but we can change the way it affects the future.

Brain scientists have discovered that neural pathways (which influence how memories are stored, among other things) get stronger the more we use them. They say, "What fires together, wires together." This means that when a person feels a certain way during a repeated situation, the brain attaches that feeling to the situation in the inner autobiography. For example, some people start getting depressed merely talking about winter, even before it has happened. Some start feeling dread when they just think about visiting the in-laws. Many children get excited about Christmas months before it arrives.

The good news is that we can gradually "rewire" our brains with new habits and new associations.

The inner autobiography is where we form a sense of power in the world; what social scientists call "locus of control." This influences whether we feel that most of the control over our lives is inside us or if we think we are mostly victims to outside powers. As a child, I saw myself as having almost no control; now, I see myself as having control over so much of my life.

Inner autobiographies set up a default mode of the Caveman, Artist, or Thinker (or some combination of these). My own inner autobiography has changed dramatically over the years. As I described in the introduction, as a child, it was a fairly dismal story. By my mid-teens, it had become a horror story. I saw myself as a victim of life, doomed to misery and a living hell.

Other people's kindness and respect helped me see that my inner autobiography was full of myths—myths that brought me down and limited me greatly. As I saw my self-concept begin to change as a result of others' kindness, I realized I could transform on purpose.

At eighteen, I began to change my inner autobiography. At nineteen, I discovered that my "Best DNA" is about creating positive transformation and motivation. I've been rewriting my inner autobiography ever since that discovery to make myself more successful, happier, and more able to get what I want in life. Despite all the adventures, growth, and even the emotional healing I've done, there remain little negative snippets of that childhood inner autobiography. I stumble upon them from time to time and work hard to rewrite them. I now see the world as having countless examples of joy, as well as pain; of triumph, as well as failure; of vitality, as well as weakness.

Henry Ford once said, "Whether you think you can, or you think you can't, you're right!" He makes a powerful point. When you take on new challenges, create an inner movie that says you can definitely succeed, and put your Artist and Thinker to work figuring out how, you set yourself up for the possibility of success. If you play this inner movie enough, and succeed sometimes, it can become part of your inner autobiography. Here's a strange paradox: Our inner movies don't have to be completely accurate to be helpful. Most people who believe they'll become celebrities don't make it. But virtually all celebrities believed that they would make it. Belief is not magic, but it's necessary. I will never become an astronaut (a childhood dream) because I toss my cookies on amusement park rides, never mind take the G forces an astronaut does. However, I created the inner movie of becoming a motivational speaker years before I began getting calls to do it.

Transformation is not a quick process. Transforming your inner autobiography may begin with a fast realization. (I hope you are having such realizations while reading this book.) However, the transformation is a gradual process that takes continued grit and energy for years. You must rewrite your inner autobiography until the story is over.

Natasha Bedingfield's inspiring pop song, "Unwritten," expresses the realization that we are the authors of our own stories:

> I am unwritten,
> Can't read my mind
> I'm undefined

I'm just beginning
The pen's in my hand
Ending unplanned

Staring at the blank page before you
Open up the dirty window
Let the sun illuminate the words
That you could not find
Reaching for something in the distance
So close you can almost taste it
Release your innovation

I encourage you to listen to the whole song. Own that ability to rewrite your life as well. Give yourself the ability to live life fully and meaningfully!

Chameleon Effect

One of the amazing things that research is uncovering is how incredibly suggestible people are. In the book, *Sway: The Irresistible Pull of Irrational Behavior*, Rom Brafman and Ori Brafman coin the term, "chameleon effect." It describes our tendency as human beings to adapt our behaviors to others' expectations—especially those who have power over us. We particularly tend to adapt to bosses' and teachers' expectations. Their expectations powerfully influence our inner movies, and therefore our motivation and performance. Also, powerful influences like these become part of our inner autobiographies over the long haul as we eventually believe that they must be right. We, of course, are constantly having a chameleon effect on others all the time as well.

Here's how it works: We form certain expectations of people or events, and we communicate those expectations with various cues, including word choice, tone of voice, speaking volume, facial expressions, body language, and the amount of attention we pay to something. People tend to adjust their behaviors to match these cues. This is especially true for those who depend on us. They may even adjust their self-concepts!

Activity 10:
Influencing Your Inner Autobiography

The more aware you are of your inner autobiography, the more you can influence it. What view of yourself and the world does your inner autobiography give you? How can you rewrite portions of it over time to make it more and more empowering? We have a lot of influence over our children and our employees. We have some influence over friends and colleagues. How can you help others, particularly those most dependent on you, to have more helpful, empowering inner autobiographies? Write your answers to help it stick in your memory.

Dov Eden, a management professor at Tel Aviv University, decided to put this to the test. He chose to use one of the most rigorous real-world environments for his research: an Israeli Army officer-training program. He set out to test what impact the chameleon effect (what he called the "self-fulfilling prophecy" dynamic) has on a leader's ability to increase performance. He defines self-fulfilling prophecy as "the process through which the expectation that an event will occur increases its likelihood of occurrence. Expecting something to happen, we act in ways that make it more likely to occur. (Note the misnomer; the prophecy does not fulfill itself. Rather, it is the prophet who, due to his expectations, acts unwittingly to bring about the expected event. This makes it appear to be self-fulfilling.)"

Professor Eden wisely guessed that "the leadership expectation effect" would activate a positive self-fulfilling prophecy in the officers in training. In this case, the leaders were four experienced training officers. He randomly designated each trainee as having high, regular, or unknown scores in "command potential." However, the training officers were told that the scores were accurate. They were also told that the scores generally have a 95 percent impact on the trainee's final course grade. Professor Eden's researchers did nothing else, except to tell the trainers to memorize the names and scores for each trainee.

The results were staggering. Those who had been randomly given the "high" scores benefited in attitude and performance. Their test scores averaged 22 percent higher than the "regular" scoring trainees. They expressed more favorable feedback on the training and in the desire for more training. The trainers had subconsciously ignited the highly-rated trainees' passion and performance through an unconscious belief that the trainees were superior. In Eden's own words:

> Raising manager expectations improves leadership which, in turn, promotes subordinate performance. The prophecy is not mysteriously self-fulfilling. Rather, manager expectations work their "magic" on subordinates by inducing managers

to provide better leadership to subordinates of whom they expect good performance. "Knowing" that in-group workers are most competent, the manager treats them as such and unwittingly fulfills his prophecy. At the same time, regarding out-group personnel as inferior, the manager expects little of them, (mis)leads them accordingly, and depresses their performance.

Activity 11:
Self-Awareness: The Chameleon Effect In Your Life

List a few examples of when someone said or did something that had a chameleon effect on you. Include examples that were helpful and some that were not. Write down what you think the effects of their chameleon effect on you were.

Since the chameleon effect is happening all the time, we might as well use it to the advantage of ourselves and others. The next chapter will demonstrate how to create a motivational chameleon effect influencing the dynamic trio, the Artist, Caveman, and Thinker.

CHAPTER 4
BE AN INNER MOVIE DIRECTOR: IGNITE PASSION AND PERFORMANCE

There are many ways to influence inner movies to ignite passion and performance. Here are the three major steps:

1. Calm the Caveman (when necessary)

2. Energize the Artist

3. Convince the Thinker

I'll start with a true story to show these steps in action, and then I'll explain more about each step in the following story. This occurred during the worst of the recession.

I hung up the phone with a sinking feeling. Yet another client canceled the consulting work I had expected to do with them. I thought to myself, I'm sunk! It's all drying up! My inner movie began to play a drama of epic proportions. I saw myself six months later, my savings gone, evicted from my home, begging friends for a handout—only to find them also on the street begging. What a dramatic inner movie my mind was creating!

I caught myself in this vicious cycle of a freeze response and put a stop to it. However, I soon began to think about my situation again, and more tragedies played out in my inner movie. In the next movie, I saw myself not only the victim of a recession, but somehow not competent enough as a professional. (This, I believe, was a fight response. My Caveman was looking for someone to blame. It wanted to kick butt and take names, even if it was my own butt.) I begin to see myself as less talented at helping others transform their company culture. I had thoughts that somehow the successes that I'd had were a fluke. I saw former clients shaking their heads, wondering why they had ever thought Bob Faw had been helpful to work with.

For two days, these vicious cycles played out in my inner movie, triggering even more negative thoughts and painful emotions. My despair and fear was affecting everything I did. I even found myself telling my sweetheart that maybe I wasn't good enough for her anymore! My Caveman was running rampant. In my mind, I was looking for someone to blame, some way to escape, and most of the time just freezing up, unable to do anything. I snapped at people who tried to help me. I ignored friendly offers of advice. In addition, I found myself escaping my depressing inner movies by watching Netflix videos nonstop. If you've ever been in this kind of situation, you know how painful it is and how hard it can be to break the vicious cycle.

On the third day, my Thinker finally got through. The Caveman had been making too much noise for me to hear it before. Cortisol (the stress hormone) had been flooding my brain so that I couldn't think creatively. Now, however, I started to think more clearly. I said to myself, "Okay Bob, we've thought about what might go wrong long enough. Now, let's look at what might go right." Then, I remembered that I have a powerful tool for doing exactly this—the "Positive Change Questions" (Goals? What works? What else?). Heck, I'd even written articles on getting through situations like this. My Caveman had been going so ballistic I hadn't been able to remember the questions.

The first question quickly brought my Artist back online. The question is, "Goals?" This helps people focus on the most important goals in their situation. So, I thought to myself, What type of work situations do I most want to have? What is important for me to create in my life during this recession? I decided that I needed at least enough money to pay the bills. As I thought more about it, I knew I needed the satisfaction and sense of purpose I get from teaching others about positive change.

My Artist got more excited as I thought about these goals. Just by playing the image of making enough money and having job satisfaction in my inner movie, my brain chemistry began to change immediately.

With increased momentum, I dove into the second question: "What works?" This helps people look at all the past successes that apply, the resources we have, and ideas that have worked. So, I began to list all of the things that I had done that had worked to help me make enough money to pay my bills and give me great job satisfaction. Even though my economic situation had not changed since three days before, I was already feeling more excited and confident about being able to make a positive change in my life. What a difference the new inner movies were already making!

Eagerly, I began exploring the third question: "What else?" This guides us to positively focus on how to build on our successful experiences with new and different ideas. So, Michael (my business partner) and I brainstormed many ideas on how to be successful in an economy where everybody seemed to be in freeze mode. It wasn't easy, but we kept refocusing our inner movies and came up with a bunch of exciting ideas. Our Artists were on fire now!

One of the things that worked well in the past, and had real potential to work during this situation, was freely sharing our ideas and enthusiasm for positive change. As a result of this brainstorming session, I began to speak to groups of professionals all over New England. Speaking is one of my Artist's favorite things, so I was feeling better and better. Speaking inspired me so much that I started providing free training to local, worthy nonprofits. I took the opportunity of our extra free time to double efforts with the clients we still had and my partner and I even did something radical that we hadn't had time to do before: We rebranded our firm. We went from boring "Organizational Growth Consulting" to the more dynamic "Matchbox Group," with the tagline, "ignite. involve.

inspire." I kept using the Positive Change Questions, and the momentum kept building. In addition, I started to write more blog posts and articles, created videos, and even authored this book. All of this had to start with positive inner movies that propelled me forward.

Years later, I look back with pride, and a little relief, at that moment of changing a vicious cycle into a vital cycle. The more I did what I loved, and focused on what I was able to do, the more helpful my inner movie became. The more helpful my inner movie became, the more confident I was in my work. These successes led to more work. To make this story even better, I purposely began to do more and more of the type of work I loved the most. Now I love my career more than I ever have.

Here are a few examples of people using positive inner movies to achieve their goals.

In politics there are examples across the political spectrum. Both President Reagan and Obama have used powerful imagery to motivate change. Speaking about the oppressive Berlin Wall, President Reagan challenged the Soviet leader, "Mister Gorbachev, tear down this wall!" Presidential candidate Obama proclaimed around the world, "Yes, we can!"

Advertising commercials work very hard to create inner movies in our minds that get us to think positively about their product. I still remember the 1970s Calgon bath oil TV commercial that shows an anxious woman stressed out by, "The traffic! The boss! The baby! The dog!" Then poof! She appears in an exotic bathtub with this water-softening product apparently making her relaxed and comfortable. By the images they show, she also apparently becomes filthy rich with very sexy legs. Powerful inner movie! Long after I'd forgotten what the product did I'd still remembered that Calgon was supposed to take you away from stress. Many commercials stick with people for years due to the power, or humor, of the images they create in our inner movies.

Around the turn of the millennium (I just love saying that!), I was consulting to a wonderful regional bank in Massachusetts. The CEO was trying to wake people up to the need of growth and change to adapt to the many new challenges facing the bank. He found that people were not motivated to change. As we talked I asked him, "What goals do you have for the bank that the people doing most of the work get excited about?" He wasn't sure, so I began talking to people across the bank. I found out that most people had a negative inner movie about big banks as not caring about the customers or employees. So, I asked them what they most loved about the bank. They talked about being good to customers and making a difference in the communities they served. When I brought this back to the CEO and his executive team, I recommended that they find ways to grow that help them do these two things better. Once we started planning this, and involving people in finding ways to improve these areas, almost everyone at the bank got on board with the change. The CEO got the growth and progress he wanted, and the people were able to enjoy being good to their customers even more.

The key to sustainable positive change is that you have to be more authentic than simply declaring that a water softener is going to help someone relax and feel sexy. You have to follow through with real changes. It's important to build on real positives and progress.

Another example was the record-breaking fundraising of the non-profit Front Door Agency in Nashua, NH. Again, we were helping out with strategic planning. One of our goals was for the strategic planning process to pay for our services—even before they started implementing the plan. After involving the board, the staff, the "customers," and even community members in discovering the Best DNA (all focusing on the positives), we received tremendous feedback, and ideas on where to best focus the Front Door's precious resources. A few months after our plan was decided on, the Front Door ran its big yearly fundraiser. I was sitting near the Development Director and she told me that the donations this year were the best ever. I smiled both in satisfaction and in triumph at my successful prediction. I can't be sure how much of their great success was due to the positive questions, but I will say that the bulk of the increased donations came from people involved in the positive-focused strategic planning.

Activity 12:
Identifying Your Successful Inner Movies

Write about a situation where your inner movie helped you succeed. Think about what you said to yourself, what you read, or what others said to you that helped you create a positive inner movie. These techniques for success are important to remember, because it's far easier and more powerful to build on your own successes than it is to learn new ideas from someone else.

I'm going to share with you some of what goes on in our brains that helps turn these positive inner movies into more success in life.

Identifying Inner Movies to Replace

If you can, notice what thoughts you might have had that caused a negative inner movie. In the future, when you notice those thoughts again, you can choose to change the inner movie with the tools I'll teach you in the next chapter.

Note: Be gentle with yourself, everybody has negative inner movies! It's normal. It's human. And it's something to learn from. If you can, when you think back to a failing situation, think of yourself gently. One way to do that is to imagine it was someone you respect a lot. This helps prevent an "F response" from occurring right now. Our Caveman can actually have an "F response" in reaction to a memory about ourselves, or even a fear we have in the moment.

Energize the Artist

The Artist gets passionate about things you find fulfilling, exciting, meaningful, and enjoyably challenging. This is so helpful in energizing higher performance! Take some time to think about the things in life that you are most passionate about; the Artist is highly active when you're engaged in those activities. Now, think about the activity you enjoy the most and feel the most satisfied with. What is it about that activity that makes you so passionate? Obviously, the more time you spend doing activities that bring passion into your life, the more you will enjoy being alive. If you can do these things in ways that help you pay your bills, even better. The Artist is very interested in the emotional side of the WIIFM (What's In It For Me) factor.

Activity 13: Energizing Your Artist

Look over the following list of ways to energize the Artist. Think of where you can use each of these items to help energize your Artist for the challenge in Activity 14. List other ideas that can energize your Artist to help self-motivate. Write down ideas for energizing other people's Artists, too, and think of who you would like to see more motivated.

Here are some ways to energize the Artist:

- Thinking about exciting goals, both short-term and long-term.

- Imagining the benefits of an idea.

- Remembering past successes. This builds the Artist's confidence, calms the Caveman, and builds a sense of emotional momentum. It also helps us get moving and pick up speed on a project.

- Thinking of examples of others who have accomplished your goal.

- Exploring creative ways to solve challenges and enjoyable ways to get to solutions.

As you work to energize your Artist, it's important to have a good portion of your creative time spent being completely positive. For example, brainstorm as many ideas as you can for solving a work challenge. During the brainstorming process, write every idea down, even the half-baked, wacko, and bizarre ones; these off-the-wall ideas often help spark great new ideas and can even turn out to be the best solutions when you look at them differently. During these brainstorming sessions, do not allow anyone to say a single negative thing—no editing or judging until the brainstorming is done. This type of creative thinking allows the Artist to truly work its magic. Once you have a great list, then get the Thinker involved to analyze and judge what is the best idea (or combination of ideas). Don't waste time talking negatively about ideas that won't work; just go for the gold.

Calm the Caveman

One important step in turning a scary situation around, as in my story, is first to calm the Caveman. Especially if the Caveman is already fully engaged in an "F response," you may need to calm the Caveman before you can energize the Artist's passion. Calming the

Caveman also enables the Thinker to be heard and to think more clearly. It's kind of like turning down the volume on your teenager's "gangsta" rap so you can think clearly and feel excited about having a great family life.

The good news is that we can influence our inner movies to calm ourselves. That's good, isn't it? This tactic is especially useful when the Caveman wants to call your boss a "jerk" or scream at your kids.

Activity 14:
Positive Change with Your Own Challenge

For the next few activities, it will be helpful for you to apply them to a current challenge of your own. Choose a situation in which you want to be more successful but are having trouble motivating yourself to do what needs to be done. It can be a small thing, like getting taxes done, or as big as my example in the recession story. Write these challenges down.

So, how do you go about this task of calming the Caveman? Following are some techniques I teach my clients for calming the Caveman so they can refocus and get motivated again. Remember: We are all as unique as fingerprints. Some things work for one person, but not for another. So take ideas, adapt them, and use any helpful techniques you already know.

Activity 15:
Calm the Caveman
Through Breathing

Breathing can calm the Caveman and allow the Thinker to refocus. If you can master the use of breathing as a calming technique, a variation of it can be helpful in almost any situation. If you practice this at least once a day for the next month you'll be able to use it at will for years to come.

1. Sit with your feet flat on the floor and your hands on your legs or a tabletop.

2. Sit up as straight as you can while still remaining comfortable. There should be no stiffness in your posture.

3. Close your eyes, if you're comfortable doing so.

4. Take a slow, deep breath until you've completely filled your lungs.

5. Exhale until all of the air is out of your lungs. Push it out.

6. Repeat slow, deep breaths with complete exhalations 3-5 times.

7. Open your eyes. Notice how much more relaxed you feel and how much more aware of your surroundings you are.

Be an Inner Movie Director: Ignite Passion and Performance

- Breathing slow, deep breaths. This is the easiest and fastest technique.

- Visualizing a calm scene, ideally a place in nature you love or some other peaceful scene.

- Thinking about the positive traits of the person you're upset with.

- Taking a break from the stressful situation. It takes about 18 minutes for an "F response" to calm down, but exercise speeds that up.

- Reframing your "Caveman comment" (what your Caveman wants you to say to someone) into a statement/question that creates a positive inner movie for yourself (and for others, if possible). See Chapter 5 for how to do this.

- Meditating, praying, or other practices that help you get centered and feel more positive.

- Exercising, stretching, dancing, and other movement that helps burn off the biochemicals released during an "F response."

- Using any or all of your senses. Some people find certain scents, music, or nurturing touch to be calming.

Convince the Thinker

In addition to calming the Caveman's fears and exciting the Artist, positive change of any type also requires convincing the Thinker. This part of the brain wants to have a clear vision of how to get to your goals. If there's too much detail, the Caveman gets bored and confused, but too little detail leaves the Thinker unconvinced. For example, when I had to change the vicious cycles of economic despair into the vital cycles of a great career, I created a few steps that I thought would lead me to my goals. I planned the first step, but I didn't worry too much about the following steps until I was ready for them. Each person's Thinker is different and requires a different blend of information. Experiment to find out how much planning is enough to make your Thinker confident, without planning so much that you lose motivation in the process. The Caveman part of our brain starts to rebel when plans get too complex.

Activity 16: Calming Your Caveman

Write down the techniques in the following list that you already do well. Also, look for ideas that you might want to try for your current challenge. Write them down someplace to remind yourself. (There are countless other calming techniques you can use.)

There are several ways to convince the Thinker:

- Listing long-term benefits for achieving a challenge.

- Talking about how you think you'll be able to achieve a new challenge (if appropriate).

- Brainstorming multiple plans.

- Analyzing the possible consequences.

- Creating a plan overview with sequenced activities on a timeline.

- Creating a detailed plan. You don't always have to follow it, but just having it ready will help get the Thinker on board.

- Coming up with contingency plans for negative consequences.

- Making a list of the pros and cons of your top ideas.

Activity 17: Calming Someone Else's Caveman

You can use some of the Caveman-calming techniques listed to help calm another person's Caveman also. For example, I may encourage someone to take a walk with me or to take a break from the situation. I may talk to them about positive traits of the person they're upset with; but be careful with this one—if they're really mad, it doesn't work until they've calmed down. I also may reframe the problem into a potential solution, as you'll learn in Chapter 5. Write down the techniques you want to try.

Some people need lots of background information and analysis to help convince the Thinker. However, people who have stronger Artist tendencies are happier with a big picture and motivating reasons, and are impatient with too much data. When motivating others, choose your approach based on what they prefer.

There are some things that both the Caveman and the Thinker like. For example, both like it when you are clear about a specific amount to accomplish. This works whether your goal is money, job satisfaction, depth of relationship, or any other goal in life. Both of these parts of the brain also like things that are clearly beneficial to all aspects of your life. For example, when I started doing more public speaking, my Thinker enjoyed the mental stimulation and potential for bringing in more work, my Caveman enjoyed the fun I had working a crowd, and my Artist thrived on the passion I felt talking about positive change.

Activity 18: Convince Your Thinker

Look over the following list of ways to convince the Thinker, and consider where you can use any of these techniques to help convince your Thinker to accomplish your current challenge. List other ideas that can help convince your Thinker and inspire self-motivation. Then, write down ideas for convincing other people's Thinkers of needed change. For example, you might tell an angry team member, "The boss looks for great team skills when she promotes people. Make sure to handle this conflict in a way that helps the team out."

Be an Inner Movie Director: Ignite Passion and Performance

Get Your A.C.T. Together

When you have the whole A.C.T. team (Artist, Caveman and Thinker) working together, you are at your best. You can tell you are in this space when you have the following characteristics:

- You feel calm about whatever challenge you're facing, but energized enough to make a difference. This means your Caveman is calm.

- You can see more than one perspective on the challenge; it's not just "my way or the highway." Understanding multiple points of view shows your Thinker is engaged.

- You use new approaches to the challenge and even want to try new things. This means your Artist is energized.

When you have your "A.C.T." together, you can make your best decisions. You will be flexible, "change-ready," have less stress, and be a more positive influence on other people. You'll also be increasingly likeable the more you are in this mode. The faster you can get your A.C.T. team to work together, the more you'll enjoy your circumstances. You'll increase passion and performance for a fulfilling and successful life.

Positive Priming: Using the Chameleon Effect on Purpose

There is another fascinating thing about how the brain works. Everything we see, think and experience primes (biases) how we respond to the next thing we encounter. For example, if you win one contest, you will understandably feel more confident entering another contest. But the confidence can also apply even when the two activities are completely unrelated. John Bargh, a psychology professor at Yale, did a fascinating experiment on this topic in regard to how people view aging. In 1996, his video recorded research participants coming to, and leaving from, a research lab. While in the lab, he exposed them to different words. Those who saw words related to being elderly tended to exit the hallway more slowly than when they'd entered. The BBC posted an interesting YouTube video of their replication of Bargh's experiment called "The Science of the Young Ones: Priming."

We are being primed all the time by everything we encounter. Positive priming is a way of purposefully creating an inner movie that activates helpful brain chemistry to prepare for a challenge. At the beginning of the book, I mentioned that we are wired with a "negativity bias." Based on our inner autobiographies, we are also already biased to think of ourselves as smart or dumb, fast or slow, confident or insecure, attractive or ugly, or creative or not, among other self-perceptions. With positive priming, we can temporarily enhance a good bias or partially counterbalance a negative one. We can set ourselves up with an "intelligence bias," "confidence bias," "creativity bias," or "open-minded bias," instead of a "loser bias" or other negative biases. Positive priming has been shown to be especially important to people needing to improve physical or relationship skills. What skills would you most like to improve with positive priming?

You might be wondering if this type of positive inner movie created by priming really can make a difference in the real world. D.F. Sewell wanted to see the impact of "directed thought" (what I see as creating an inner movie) on swimmers in 1996. He asked swimmers to focus on various things while they swam, and he found that the swimmers who were told to "use positive imagery of swimming smoothly and powerfully" improved the most. This was even more helpful than focusing on technique.

Priming experiments have been repeated, in various ways, hundreds of times, and it is both startling and exciting to see how much we can influence ourselves and others. Our brains are being primed all the time, whether we are aware of it or not. If events and words around us are priming us, we might as well prime ourselves on purpose. Directing inner movies is purposefully priming the brain. You can direct your inner movies to increase your probability of success at any given venture. It's not magic. It's not mystical. It's brain science.

A number of motivational psychologists have asked the same question: "Which gives better results: focusing on positives or negatives?"

Four researchers at the University of Wisconsin decided to find out. They used one of America's most popular adult sports, bowling, to do the research. The experiment involved monitoring the scores of low-skilled bowlers in four leagues over a few months, and two leagues showed something startling. One league had been asked to track only what they did right and focus on doing those things more; another league had been asked to track only the mistakes and focus on avoiding those errors in the future. While both teams improved, the team tracking what they did right had 100 percent greater improvement than the team that was tracking its mistakes!

10:1 Positive:Negative High-Performing Ratio

We've learned that focusing just on positives will help us more than focusing just on negatives. But what's the ideal balance of the two? Sometimes you have to be able to clearly identify when something fails. Is there an ideal ratio between positive and negative talk?

Social psychologist Marcial Losada took on this mathematically complex challenge. With Barbara Fredrickson he experimented to find out the ideal positive-negative ratio for individual "flourishing." With Emily Heaphy, he investigated business teams to see how much positivity was needed to be high-performing. They used sixty strategic management teams of eight people from one company. Each of the teams had been thoroughly assessed to determine whether they were low-performing, medium-performing, or high-performing. Then they were observed in a capture lab developing their annual strategic plans. The researchers analyzed everything they said. They counted up all the positive things, and the negatives as well. What they found was fascinating.

The researchers found a strong correlation between positive language and performance. Low-performing teams communicated one positive for every three negatives, or a ratio of 1:3, while medium-performing teams averaged 2:1. That's six times as positive just to be medium! High-performing teams scored about 6:1. What an amazing difference.

There were upper limits of effective positivity for both teams and individuals. Individuals they found at 12:1 did not adapt well enough to changes. Purely thinking positive will end in disaster almost as surely as only being negative, even if it might be a more enjoyable ride of the tracks.

Our lessons? We need lots of positivity to be expansive, enthusiastic and creative. Plus, we need enough negativity to face the hard truths. Most importantly, we need to have the right ratio. I recommend aiming for 10:1 ratio—to speak and think positively roughly 10 times as often as you do negatively. I find this a helpful goal both as an individual and as a team. Even if you only reach 6 times as much positivity, you'll still be doing well. Positives are topics like goals, what's working so far, new ideas for the future, and positive reinforcement for other people's contributions. In this case, negatives would include statements like "that won't work," "we can't afford that," "that project failed," and "I don't know how." Ten percent of the time we do have to identify and talk about the "hard truths," but then we need to get back to talking about solutions. This 10 percent of the time should not include things like shaming, cynicism, name-calling. These are corrosive and are not about hard-truths, just distorted Caveman-talk.

Positive:Negative Marriage Ratio

While we're on the topic of ideal balance, what about marriage? In 1999, Researchers John Gottman and Sybil Carrere decided to find out by asking a group of newlyweds to talk about their first conflicts. After watching these couples for years, they discovered that most couples with sustainable marriages had something in common: They showed five times the amount of positive emotions regarding their partner than they showed negative emotions when discussing the conflict. And this was while talking about a conflict! In everyday life, I suspect the ratio should be even higher. How often is it, though? I've worked a lot harder at being positive since reading this startling research. I aim for 10:1 in the love department, too.

By the way, the couples that didn't have enough positivity split up, or even worse they end up with what I call a "lifetime of mutual hostage taking."

Using Positive Priming

I love the bowling and swimming examples because they show that priming is best done before and during a challenge. For positive priming to work effectively, you must acknowledge the negatives that you need to, then quickly move back to an inner movie of what you do want to do.

My challenge to you is to replace the inner movies that bring you down (as you are able) with ones that increase confidence. Here's my Dancing story, which shows one area I've used priming to help me.

Activity 19: Improving Your Positive:Negative Ratio

When I apply the 10:1 ratio to my life, I think of all of my interactions with a specific person. Positives can include a smile, a pat on the back, words of encouragement, helpful ideas, and anything else that is about helping that person move forward versus critiquing the past. Where would you like to improve your ratio? List things you can say to focus more on positive goals, ideas, and affirmations when your Caveman may want to start swinging its club.

When I was twenty-two years old, I was struggling to overcome a fear of being rejected by women. While visiting my brother, the two of us decided to go dancing. He took me to a hopping Latin dance club. I was already nervous about going to the club, but my intimidation doubled when I realized we were the only blonde people in the room. To make it even worse, many of the men dancing here were far better dancers than we were. Immediately, an inner movie began playing in my mind. I saw myself sitting in the corner all night, dejected, laughed at by all of the women around me.

Since I anticipated this reaction, I had prepared an inner movie the night before to counteract this. I decided that a rejection did not change who I was; the only thing that would change was my courage. Having the guts to ask became a prize in itself! While this was a powerful inner movie, I wanted a plan that supported it, so I decided to keep at it until I'd asked at least twenty women to dance. That would take a lot of courage.

I played this scene in my mind several times until I was semi-confident about it. That evening at the dance club was not the story of Bob being rejected; it was the story of Bob confidently asking twenty women to dance. That way, I felt that I succeeded regardless of how the women responded.

The moment of truth had arrived. I looked across the sea of gyrating salsa dancers and saw a number of women leaning against one wall, watching the dancing. Putting on my friendliest smile (I hoped it wasn't a grimace), I boldly walked up to the first woman.

"Would you like to dance?" I managed to ask in a semi-relaxed way. She raised her nose and scoffed at me. Before the word "no" had left her mouth, I had moved on to the second woman. I received five more variations of "get lost" and was beginning to suspect that I was going to reach the number twenty very quickly. I asked the seventh woman if she would like to dance one dance with me, and I almost moved on before I realized that she had said, "Sure."

Pleasantly surprised, I led her to the dance floor. My dance style could easily be described as enthusiastic, but I was no Fred Astaire. For me, dancing is about the interaction between two people. Unfortunately, my new dance partner, as attractive as she was, stared at the wall behind my shoulder the whole dance. I decided, heck, I still have thirteen more no's to go, so I might as well try to find someone more fun to dance with.

I thanked my partner and went back to the wall of leaning women. Four invitations later, a delightful young lady gave me an enthusiastic "Yes!" She was playful and fun, and we danced the night away.

Before this experience, I had been dominated by inner movies of "I'll be rejected," "I'm not a good dancer," "I'm not attractive or smooth enough," "I'll be humiliated at the dance in front of the cool people," and "Knowing me, I'll spend the evening leaning against the wall," among other crippling scenes. These wreaked havoc on my social life.

By transforming my inner movie to "I'm courageous enough to collect twenty rapid no's," I ended up dancing a whole lot more. I also ended up dating a lot more. By focusing my inner movie on "I dance for fun, not to impress," I gave myself more freedom to experiment and learn.

From that point on, when I went dancing, anytime I felt nervous I replayed these inner movies and used that strategy. As a result, I learned how to actually listen to the beat, picked up a bunch of fun moves, took lessons, and over time became one of the "cool" people on the dance floor. This strategy has worked extremely well for me in dancing and many other places in life. As you can imagine, my self-perception of my dance skills in my inner autobiography has been dramatically rewritten. I've had so much fun, and been complimented so many times while dancing, that now I start out confident and upbeat.

I've used the same type of inner movie and the same strategy of asking twenty people to help with job seeking, selling my consulting services, and any other place where "rejections" are merely a normal part of the journey to success.

The more you positively prime yourself, the easier it gets to prime for new situations. I use priming now in many varied circumstances, such as: business meetings, social situations where I have some anxiety, sales meetings, difficult conversations with loved ones, calling customer support (I tend to get impatient and hang up too quickly), talking with people about controversial topics like politics or religion, and countless other situations when my Caveman is creating angry or anxious inner movies.

Positively Priming Others

As we learned with the chameleon principle, we affect other people's inner movies. Because of this, it's important to positively prime others on purpose, particularly if you are a business executive, a parent, a teacher, or a leader of any type.

For example, when I want people to tap into their true passions, I ask them to share a story of their "peak moments" in their companies. It might be helping a customer, solving a challenge, being part of a great team, or coming up with a new idea. This primes them to be more passionate about improving their performance, being strong team players, and embracing new changes. I also ask them to talk with their partners or colleagues about their greatest accomplishments at work. This primes them with the confidence to help them take on their next challenges and helps them see how good, smart, creative, and strong they are. We all have our weaknesses, but talking about those weaknesses only motivates a small percentage of people; focusing on positivity is much more productive. And since I find that people love talking about their successes, this type of priming also helps build rapport. If they don't have successes in the area I need them to focus on, we discuss stories of others who have been successful.

I primed myself this way, too. When I first started my business in the 1980s, work was so slow. I could only eat rice and beans at times. I kept thinking of Thomas Edison, who made well over a thousand attempts before he found a way to make a long-burning light bulb. When I've failed, I've reminded myself that Abraham Lincoln lost more elections than he won—and he still became one of the greatest presidents. I've used these same stories to prime others.

Here's another example of where you can apply the chameleon effect for positive motivation: If you see your employees (or children, for that matter) as full of good potential, they're far more likely to succeed than if you think of them as failures. Even if you don't verbalize what you think of them, your unconscious body language, tone of voice, and even actions send them repeated messages that they pick up. These signals influence their inner movies, which guide their beliefs and actions, too. It can be a vicious cycle, or a vital cycle, depending on how you interact with them. A simple, but powerful, positive change technique is to bring to mind people's successes and strengths before being with them. This will help influence you in order to influence them in a more positive way.

Be an Inner Movie Director

Congratulations! If you've practiced priming, you're already an inner movie director. Now, you just need to keep getting better. Choose an area of your life that you want to improve. Like the bowlers who improved quickly through focusing on positivity, keep thinking of how to direct your next energizing inner movie. Afterward, analyze only what worked well. Then, practice again. If you do this every day for the next thirty days, you will have ingrained this new skill set into your long-term memory, along with a powerful new confidence. At that point, start focusing on negatives in the right balance (10:1) to help yourself grow.

Activity 20: Priming Practice

1. Think of a situation where you'd like to be more confident. Start small to make practice easier. For example, you might want more confidence asking for resources on a project, asking your significant other for a favor, or bringing up a challenging topic with a coworker (or even scarier, a family member).

2. As you play out approaching that situation in your inner movie, simply notice the useless inner movies that begin to play. Don't try to change them yet, just write them down as if they have titles (similar to how I referenced the dancing story). Remind yourself that it is completely normal and healthy to have these inner movies—even if they're not always helpful.

3. Without editing out any ideas, take two to five minutes to brainstorm as many helpful scenarios as you can think of that you could play in your inner movies. Write down everything—even the crazy, wacko ones; writing funny or violent ones helps the Caveman discharge some energy. Just make sure to also write ones that could help everyone involved come out looking and feeling good.

4. Pick the top one to three inner movies that you think would be the most likely to help you the next time you enter the situation you chose.

5. Practice one of them in your mind. Talk confidently with supportive friends about how you will put it into practice.

6. Once this inner movie feels real enough, try it in the real situation. I find that playing it a number of times right before I enter the situation is the most helpful. Then, during the situation I can quickly "glance" at the inner movie to bolster my confidence as needed.

7. Keep experimenting with this technique until you start getting successes. Then, keep building on what you've done well.

Choose Positive Goals

Positive goals make more energizing inner movies, because negative goals such as "stop smoking" or "stop being a couch potato" tend to bring morale down by creating a continuous movie of the behavior you want to stop. Creating positive goals of "being alive for my grandchildren" or "being able to run five miles" tend to bring about more passion and excitement. Positive goals also tend to direct your mind toward the things that can make you healthier, rather than just stopping a few things that make you unhealthy. I'll take the example of smokers who want to be healthier. They can make a goal of improving their physical endurance, or increasing the number of people who will date them, or the amount of years they will live healthily. In addition to quitting smoking, this will energize them to find a running partner, to join a yoga class, or hit the gym more often, as opposed to just getting a nicotine patch. For people who keep thinking, "I want to quit smoking" they're accidentally playing an inner movie of smoking (just with a red line over the cigarette). The image of the cigarette rekindles the urge to smoke every time it plays.

This works the same for business goals. I've worked with quality managers to change their goals from "reducing waste by ten percent" to "increasing quality through out by ten percent." It's far more motivating to give input in to increasing quality production. When people ask about how to reduce waste, it often triggers the Caveman's blaming response and people start pointing fingers.

Amp Up the Energy with Positive Change Questions

I've developed and refined three questions over years of consulting, training, and research that are designed to ignite passion and performance through activating the A.C.T. team in helpful ways.

The first question, "Goal?" enables the Thinker to focus the Caveman and Artist on the direction you need to move toward.

The second question, "What works?" calms the Caveman by playing inner movies of strengths and resources that you already have. It also taps into the positive energy of the Artist by increasing confidence through playing inner movies of past successes. As an extra bonus, it brings up great ideas that the Artist grabs onto and builds upon.

The third question "What else?" not only energizes the creativity of the Artist, it bypasses the Caveman's typical questions of "What's wrong with them?" or the depressing "gap analysis." By talking about what else you can do in addition to your strengths, you're looking forward to solutions rather than back at "What's missing?" "Who's not up to speed?" and all the other typical questions that tend to kick off a stormy blame game—even in your own head.

Energizing Effect of the Positive Change Questions

My clients often tell me that we come up with far more ideas, far more quickly, when we use the Positive Change Questions. I also hear that the process is energizing and fun for folks. Sometimes, clients are able to come up with ideas that regular problem-solving couldn't achieve. If you completed Activity 21, did you notice the energy you felt after using the questions? How about the number of ideas you were able to come up?

I've used the chameleon effect to prime my brain for business success. Earlier, I told you how I prepared for my presentation at a Monster.com conference. Now, I'll tell you how priming my inner movie saved the day again; this time as I approached the stage, in my Priming the Inner Movie for Public Speaking: Monster story.

I was just about to get on stage and speak to the 140 telesales people from Monster.com about Language of Influence. I had four hours ahead of me to help them understand the concepts, learn some skills, and motivate them to use these skills in their jobs. As I began to walk toward the stage, one of the trainers who works for Monster came up and quipped with a wry grin, "Good luck, Bob, I can't keep their attention for ten minutes!"

Yikes! Instantly, my inner movie changed from one about my successful first words to one of despair! As I slowly forced myself to walk toward the stage, my inner movie was playing out a scene of chaos. I saw salespeople talking over me, people sending text messages incessantly, bored trainees walking out in the middle of my training, and horror of horrors, people ignoring my fun activities. Worst of all, I saw myself standing hopeless on the stage, completely powerless to stop it all.

Halfway to the stage, I realized what was happening. I shook my head and said to myself, Remember who I am! So, I began to play a new inner movie. I recalled my "Power Speaker" inner movie, and I played a wonderful scene that had occurred after a presentation I did on Language of Influence at Odyssey Healthcare in Dallas, Texas. Then, the scene playing in my mind was one of happy people shaking my hand at the end of my presentation; folks saying, "Thank you for the insights! You were really inspiring" and a man approaching with tears in his eyes, saying, "I will be a better father now, not just a better leader!"

With this inner movie playing, I felt my confidence returning with every step I took toward the stage. My shoulders straightened. The lightheadedness that had invaded my mind was changing back to mental clarity and excitement. My Caveman, of course, who was watching my inner movie, began to think that these sales people were my old friends from Odyssey, and calmed down. Just as important, my Artist was now back online, eager to get up and talk to the audience. My Thinker began to purposefully alternate my inner movie between scenes from Odyssey and the first few words I planned to say on stage. As I climbed the stairs to the stage, I was full of excitement and confidence—and it was authentic confidence, not faked. I stood tall, my arms spread wide, and spontaneously let out an excited, booming "Hello, Monster!" The crowd roared back its happy response. All my fear dropped away, and my passion for speaking began to run the show. The four hours flew by in a flurry of excitement and engagement.

If I had not directed my inner movie using this priming technique, that moment of crisis would have caused my carefully planned speech to be a flop. I have used the same inner movie many times to help me in my public speaking, and I've taught it to thousands of others looking to improve their presentation skills. I've also found that positive priming is far more helpful than worrying about "ums," "ers," or anything that creates an inner movie of what I don't want to have happen.

Activity 21:
Positive Change Questions for Planning Improvement

Write down your responses.

1. Goal? Write down a positive goal you have for yourself.

2. What works?

> A. Make a list of all the things you are already doing, as well as the knowledge, skills, and resources you already have that are helping you toward this goal.

> B. Pick three to five things from your list that you feel are the most helpful. Strengthen your commitment to continue doing them by writing down how you can do these more often or even better than you've done them in the past.

3. What else?

> A. Brainstorm ideas on your own, with others, and with the assistance of your favorite search engine (e.g., Google). List any idea that has the remotest possibility of helping you toward your goal. Don't do any critical editing at this time, just write it all down.

Be an Inner Movie Director: Ignite Passion and Performance

B. Pick a few of the most interesting and easiest for you to do. Start one of them today or at least sometime this week. Once this idea has become a habit for you, add a new one. The reason I suggest picking an easy idea to start with is that success builds confidence and confidence builds success. By adding one new habit at a time, you also build that sense of accomplishment and a desire to continue. That's a great inner movie! If we start too many things at one time, we tend to get overwhelmed. Feeling overwhelmed often leads to the freeze response, which starts a vicious cycle. One of the keys to positive change is making the change process itself as positive as the end result.

4. Action

A. Brainstorm a list of ways to direct a motivational inner movie for your goal. For example, write things that you will gain and any other benefits of achieving the goal.

B. Pick the most motivating and easiest-to-accomplish idea. (You can always improve it or change it later.)

C. Play this scene in your inner movie with as much detail as you can. Make this a powerful inner movie by imagining the wonderful feelings that you will have when you accomplish your goal. Think of the good things that others are likely to say to you and envision the opportunities that will open up for you as a result of achieving your goal. Play this inner movie for yourself at least three times a day.

As you can imagine, practicing priming with this inner movie before public speaking events has also rewritten part of my inner autobiography. I've transformed from seeing myself as a painfully shy boy terrified of rejection and looking stupid into an exuberant, confident man who loves to speak to groups.

Think about your inner autobiography. What is one long-held belief about yourself and the world that is holding you back? It may be something that started as a child, or it may have resulted from an experience as an adult. What would you like that part of your inner autobiography to say about you instead? Imagine yourself in that new way of being.

On a personal level, I've seen thousands of people transform positively. One example comes immediately to mind. I was in Chicago to co-present with a client about his successful leadership development program that I had helped with. The night before our joint presentation we were out for some of Chicago's best steak and beer. When I told him how much fun I have presenting, he shared that he sees presentations as "just something to get through." I told him that if he plays a different inner movie, it might change the way he feels about speaking. After a few beers and a lot of great brainstorming, he said he'd try out the new perspective of presenting. He had more fun the next day, and it gets even better. A few years later, at a different restaurant, Pat shared that since that day in Chicago he'd enjoyed presenting more and more. He's liking it so much that now he searches for opportunities, and sees how it is giving him great exposure that is helping him with his career. This was confirming evidence for the technique of looking for what we enjoy in something, and playing that in our inner movie. It can be a huge help in getting better at it.

Now you've learned about using positive priming for motivation. The next chapter will take you to the next level of mastery. I'll teach more powerful tools for your motivational tool box.

Be an Inner Movie Director: Ignite Passion and Performance

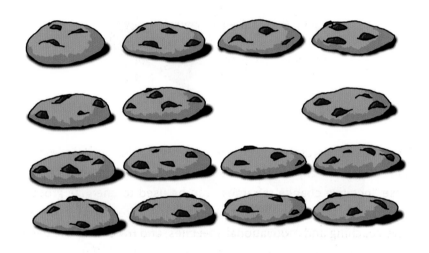

CHAPTER 5
MOTIVATIONAL LANGUAGE TOOLS

This chapter shares more powerful communication techniques that calm the Caveman, energize the Artist, and convince the Thinker; these "positive change reframes" can be used to energize groups, entire organizations, and even yourself. I use the techniques in executive coaching and motivational speeches, and my clients use these skills at work and at home. The reframes are some of the most concrete and easy to learn tools, which my clients love.

Positive Change Reframes

What do you see when you look at the drawing on the previous page? Every time I ask this question, some people in the audience excitedly yell, "Cookies!" And every time, others in the audience yell, "There's a cookie missing!" Both of these answers are true, and yet each creates very different responses. Simply seeing "cookies" creates excitement, anticipation, and smiles. Seeing that "a cookie is missing" creates suspicion, frowns, and readiness to blame. And this is just looking at a simple drawing.

Positive change reframing is the art of transforming a negative "Caveman comment" into words that calm the Caveman and energize the Artist's passion. Because of our "negativity bias," we humans have a tendency to blurt out directions focusing too much on what to avoid, stop, or prevent. This can make very confusing and counter productive inner movies. For example, even after a lot of progress had been made on improving leadership, I heard a CEO tell his staff, "We're still not doing it right." He accidentally created inner movies of complete failure. His staff started protesting and defending themselves, instead of looking for ways to improve.

Positive change reframing purposely uses specific words and tone of voice to create the inner movie and actions you need. These words and tones are blended to create an inner movie that inspires people to move towards your goals. For example the CEO could have said, "We made some real progress, particularly in some areas. Let's keep improving our ability to motivate our people." His staff are more likely to feel appreciated for the progress they'd made, and to have inner movies of ways to improve.

Thinking negative Caveman comments and wanting to say them to other people is completely, 100 percent natural and okay. Actually saying those comments out loud, or repeating them in your inner movie, is another matter altogether. If you want to become unpopular and miserable, say these negative Caveman comments repeatedly to yourself and others. If you want to motivate and lead by example, use a positive reframe.

The point is this: Be gentle with yourself, and accept the fact that it is natural to have negative thoughts and urges. But remember that you are responsible for what you do and say, regardless of the comments the Caveman wants you to make. If you want to succeed and form good relationships, use positive change reframes.

What does a reframe look like? Here are some examples of great reframes clients of ours came up with at a Leadership University put on by my firm ran for a client of ours. I taught them to motivate themselves and others using positive change reframes. Once they'd done the reframes out of class, I asked them to write down the urge (what the Caveman wanted to say), the reframe they used, and the result of using the reframe.

Example 1

Urge: I got a same-day email from the nonprofit I volunteer for, reminding me of a meeting that evening. I was really surprised because I didn't remember hearing about it in advance. My urge was to say, "You need to give people more notice for these things."

Reframe: I emailed my contact and said, "I'm so sorry if there was a miscommunication, but I'm unaware of the meeting and away on a family trip this week. Although I won't be able to attend tonight, I will be sure to follow up with you next week to see if there are any action items pertinent to me."

Result: The meeting was rescheduled!

Example 2

Urge: I wanted to tell an employee to forget about doing the task I assigned him, since it was due and he hadn't started it.

Reframe: I asked him, "What challenges are holding you back from completing this task?"

Results: We worked together to solve the problem that was keeping the task from being completed.

Example 3

Urge: The line for the Winnie the Pooh ride at Disney was crazy long, and I wanted to tell my family that it was a ridiculous waste of time.

Reframe: I noticed that there were lots of hands-on activities for the kids to entertain themselves while we were waiting in line. So I said, "It seems like we're going to be waiting for a while. Let's explore this waiting area and see all of the fun things that are here."

Result: Even though it was still a significant investment of time, we all had a great time while we waited for our honey pot to arrive.

Positive Change Reframe Story

I want you to imagine that we have a Caveman Hunter (like the Crocodile Hunter) guide who is going to take us into someone's mind.

This way we can see reframes being created by the Thinker, and their affects on the Caveman, and Artist. We have a brave guide who will lead us into the mind of Joe. Joe is a software engineer who volunteered to allow us into his mind for a while so we can see his inner movie, Artist, Caveman, and Thinker up close. This way, we can see how reframes can ignite passion and performance. The reframes in the story are in italics.

> **Guide:** Come on, mates. If we find the Caveman in his natural habitat, we'll be the first to see him in the wild! Careful now. I need to follow these neuron paths leading from the ear canal all the way to the amygdala. Keep your head down. (looking around) Don't touch that neuron. It's live with electricity.
>
> Oh! I see something. There's the Caveman. He's staring at a huge screen, which must be the inner movie. Oh, and next to him are the Thinker and the Artist. The Thinker's moving a giant steering wheel, guiding Joe's feet. There's also a giant

megaphone—that must be how they get Joe to say what they want him to say. And, look at that! There is a giant pair of gloves that the characters can put their whole arms into, to move Joe's arms for him. Let's move closer and see what's playing in the inner movie.

Okay, it looks like Joe is going into a meeting room. I can see five—no, six people in the room already. There's Joe's boss at the head of the table. Uh-oh! His boss just told them all that there were a lot of errors in the last project, and he wants to know who made the mistakes. The Artist is hiding, and—crikey!—the Caveman is getting huge and ferocious looking. He's grabbing the megaphone.

Caveman: Attack! Attack!

Joe: (blurting out forcefully) It was the fault of the research group! They gave us the wrong information!

Guide: Uh-oh, now the guy from the research group is pointing his finger at Joe and saying it's Joe's fault. Looking for blame isn't helping this team at all!

Thinker: (coaching Joe) The blame game is killing us, Joe. Relax, take a breath. First-time projects always have errors. The point here should be *what have we accomplished, and what do we need to do to fix the errors and move on?*

Guide: That's great. The Thinker's reframe is energizing the Artist and calming the Caveman.

Joe: (taking a deep breath) Well, actually, *I think the research guys have done a great job. We just need to work out the bugs.*

How about finding out what has worked so we can learn from each other? Then, we can focus on making the project better. I know there are a few things I can do to help it.

Guide: Fantastic! When Joe's Thinker is online, he can do some great reframes. The research guy is smiling now, and even the boss has stopped scowling. Look at that—the research guy is now talking about some good things Joe did!

Artist: (standing up and yelling) I have some great ideas!

Joe: Let's brainstorm some ideas. I've got some to get us started.

Guide: Whew! We've changed from a blame storm to a brainstorm. This will go a whole lot better. At least the Caveman has calmed down again, and the Artist is getting really creative.

The meeting is over. It looks like we're getting ready to leave. What's wrong? The Caveman is cowering.

Caveman: Boss coming!

Guide: The Caveman was really paying attention. I didn't even notice the boss coming toward Joe. The boss patted Joe on the shoulder and told him he liked the way he changed the mood of the meeting. The Caveman has quieted again, and the Artist is beaming.

Ah, we're getting to Joe's cubicle now. I'm curious to see what happens to these characters while Joe works. Crikey! Look at all those emails Joe has to answer. And most of them are labeled "urgent." And the Caveman is frozen—he looks like a deer caught in headlights.

Guide: That's incredible! The Caveman's fear of being overwhelmed has frozen all three of them. Ah, I see: Joe's inner movie is showing potential future outcomes, including a missed dinner and faces of angry coworkers for not getting a response back on time. That explains the Artist, Caveman, and Thinker looking like statues.

Thinker: (starting to move and taking a few deep breaths) Let's just take one thing at a time.

Guide: Nicely done! Did you see the way the Thinker reframed that overwhelming pile into just looking at one thing at a time? They're all moving now—slowly, but they're moving.

Joe: *Okay, which do I need to do first?*

Guide: Impressive! Now that Joe is prioritizing his e-mails, he's getting a lot done pretty quickly. Oh, look, Joe's boss asked him to fix some software bugs. I wonder if that is going to freak out his Caveman? The Thinker looks stuck, but look at the Artist switching on a light bulb—and leaping into creative action.

Artist: Playtime! Move out of the way, the master is at work! Okay, you little software bug, come to Papa.

Guide: Look at him go when his Artist is at the controls! The Caveman is relaxed, and the Thinker looks proud.

Well folks, it looks like our time is up. I hope you enjoyed the chance to see inside someone's mind. I certainly learned a lot about positive change reframes and how the Artist, Caveman, and Thinker are affected by them. I see how important the right words and tone of voice are in helping people be productive together, and Joe even used reframes to help himself get focused and calm down. I hope you and your internal Caveman, Thinker, and Artist enjoyed the trip, too!

Activity 22: When to Use Positive Change Reframes

Positive change reframes are very helpful to use with self-talk, and they're also useful when influencing others. Write about two different areas in your life where positive change reframes would be helpful to you. Create a reframe for each of these areas that might help you direct better inner movies. Feel free to adapt some of the examples given in the following table.

As this story illustrates, positive change reframes are one of the best tools for motivation. Joe changed his own behavior in the meeting from defensive and blaming, to giving credit and looking for a solution. His reframe also helped others to calm down and start contributing ideas. I've seen many of our clients become seen as team players, and people to rely on, as they replace blaming with positive change reframes. Joe also got himself out of feeling overwhelmed, and became productive, by reframing his e-mails with prioritization.

Also, his productivity soared as his Artist saw the "debugging" task as a fun challenge to solve. I hope you can see yourself getting these kinds of results using positive change reframes.

Here are a number of examples of reframes you might use to motivate yourself:

If you feel like saying something like this:	You might try reframing it to something like this:
How could I have been so dumb?	What can I learn from this to help me next time? What will I do differently in the future?
I could never accomplish that.	What would I have to do to accomplish that? What skills and abilities do I have that will help?
I'm not good at that.	Here are examples of where I have been good at that (list true examples).
That person is much better than me at (x).	I can do it well enough. That's all I need. What resources do I have to help me do it better?
That's too scary!	I'll do it to prove that I have the courage, regardless of whether I succeed or not.
I can't think of how to do this.	If I could figure it out, what ways would I come up with to do it?

Motivating Other People

As we've discussed, we influence people around us every day with every interaction. Unfortunately, we sometimes influence people away from doing what we want without even realizing it. I bet you can think of some examples of times that no matter how much you told somebody to stop doing something, they kept doing it. You may have been accidentally creating the exact movie in their heads that you didn't want them viewing.

Think about it: If you tell a child, "Don't jump on the bed!" you've just created a delightful movie of all the fun of jumping on the bed. Or, think about the effects of a manager or coach telling her team, "Don't screw up!" What is she doing to their inner movies? They are having "F responses" due to the many images of failure and the terrible results of that failure. By creating these negative inner movies, she makes it necessary for them to have to overcome what she said. Then, they have to reframe it in their own minds with what they need to do right. Where are you accidentally forcing your team, your children, or yourself to have to work extra hard just to be successful? Where can you reframe your own self-talk to energize yourself for positive change, instead of forcing yourself to overcome Caveman "F responses"?

Activity 23:
Build Your Skill: Creating Positive Change Reframes

In order to help yourself learn the skill of creating positive change reframes, take some time to create ten more reframes that will help motivate you to take action toward your goals. Write these down.

Any time you reframe a situation to motivate others, remember to use a tone of voice that calms or energizes the person you're talking to. Tone of voice is often even more important than what you say, and the more your Artist is energized and/or your Thinker is focused on solutions, the easier it is to speak with a genuinely positive tone of voice. The Caveman, on the other hand, is constantly watching for anger or condescension in another person's tone of voice.

When reframing a situation, I sometimes take a moment to tell myself (create an inner movie) of something good about the person I'm talking to before using the reframe. That usually makes the reframe more effective. Here are a number of examples of reframes you might use to help motivate others; a list of potential reframes for a variety of situations is also available at energizeperformance. com:

If you feel like saying something like this:	You might try reframing it to something like this:
Why do you ask such stupid questions?	What can I do to make this easy to understand?
Why are you always late these days?	You used to be more prompt. What can we do to help you be prompt again?
You get irritated so easily with your teammate!	(in a calm voice) Focus on how to stay calm to help the conversation stay productive.
Stop going behind my back to get things done.	I can help you succeed when you include me in your conversations.
Stop texting me; I'm busy at work.	Can we talk after work? I'd like to focus on work now so I can focus on you later.

I have no idea. No one tells me anything.	Good question, let's find that out together. I'd like to know as well.
Brush your teeth, or they'll rot out of your head.	Keep your smile attractive and your breath fresh with regular brushings.
Don't be so negative.	Focusing on a positive 10:1 ratio will help us be a high performance team.

Activity 24: Build Your Skill in Influencing Others

1. Pick the reframe(s) from the list of examples that you think will motivate others.

2. Create and write ten new reframes that will help you be more effective.

3. Put a note in your calendar to reframe three things every day for the next thirty days. By the end of the month, that skill will be hardwired into your long-term memory. (Make sure to create at least one reframe for yourself and one reframe for others.)

4. Check out the free video and blog posts on reframing at energizeperformance.com (search for "reframe").

Activity 25: Creating Reframes Together

I co-design reframes with my clients, and their input helps create reframes that are even more successful and sustainable than if I created them on my own. Get together with your team, family, or group, and make a list of Caveman-type comments that are detrimental to you all. Then, reframe them together to make more energizing and helpful statements that will help you all move forward together.

CHAPTER 6
ACTION! BECOMING A MASTER OF MOTIVATION

If you truly want to become a master of motivation, work this chapter! Don't just read it, work it. You will easily gain one hundred times more from doing the activities than reading about them. Learning to drive takes practice, and so does learning to motivate.

I hope you've come away from the previous chapters with nuggets of fascinating ideas and feel ready to use some of the tools. I'd like to share a story illustrating how many of these concepts and tools can be put to use, then we'll look at how to put more of these into action in your own life and plan for future skill growth.

This story blends together true accomplishments I've seen clients achieve over the years. I dedicate the Master of Motivation story to those people who have truly inspired me.

As CEO, Sally was the voice of Tiger Media. She knew that a merger with Diamond Media would be a great strategic move and planned to present her ideas in a meeting that afternoon. But Sally needed to con-

vince not only her board members and executives, but also the uptight owner of Diamond Media, Annika Strum.

On her way to the meeting, she saw Hiro, her head of operations, and Jane, her head of Sales, talking animatedly outside of Sally's office. As she got closer, she could see that Hiro was trying to calm Jane down.

When Jane saw Sally coming, she whirled on her. "That...beast! She is driving me crazy!" Sally quickly opened her office door and ushered them inside.

She calmly directed, "Take a deep breath, Jane, and let me know what's going on."

Jane, her face red, forced herself to calm down—then said one word with the expression she used when picking up dog waste: "Annika!"

Sally frowned; Annika had flown in just for this meeting. If she and Jane fought, it had the potential to kill the whole deal.

Hiro chuckled and quipped, "Jane's in an Annika Panicka!"

Jane spluttered, "I literally wanna kill that woman!"

Hiro cut in with a soothing voice and explained to Sally, "Annika showed up at 7:00 this morning demanding to see all of Jane's sales reports for the last three years, as well as her forecasts."

"She didn't even say 'good morning'!" Jane broke in angrily. "She just started demanding things like I was some naughty child or something. And the whole time it looked like she was sucking on a lemon!" Jane made a squished up face, mocking Annika. Hiro started laughing, then Jane did as well. This helped calm Jane a bit.

Action! Becoming a Master of Motivation

Sally intervened firmly but calmly. "I'm sorry that happened, Jane. I'll be running the meeting today, and later I'll privately let Annika understand the right way to get information from us in the future. I know it's hard given how insulting her behavior felt, but Jane, will you do your best to calm your Caveman and be ready to contribute?"

Jane hesitated, then nodded, "I'll keep focusing on the good things about her. I know how to change my inner movie."

Sally nodded appreciatively and glanced at her watch, "We have to get going; the meeting starts in two minutes."

As they walked into the huge conference room with floor-to-ceiling windows, they could see that Annika had moved in with tall stacks of paper on either side of her like fortifications. Annika had even taken Sally's usual seat at the head of the table. Sally could sense Jane starting to stir angrily and heard her grumble under her breath about the "Annika Invasion."

Ignoring this, Sally sweetly said, "Good morning, Annika," and smoothly sat down at the foot of the table with dignity. By doing so, she subtly made it the new head of the table. Sally then calmly stated, "Our goal today is to look at the benefits of a possible merger between our two firms."

"To see if there's a problem that should keep us from even doing it at all," Annika interrupted curtly.

Sally smiled at her, "The due diligence is the next step. Let's see if there are enough potential advantages to see if we want to get to that stage." She moved on quickly before Annika could interrupt again. "To begin with, we're going to do some brainstorming about all the potential *advantages." She paused, then added firmly, "At this stage, we will only come up with positive points."*

Annika's lemon-eating expression intensified, but Sally continued quickly, "We can get a lot of positive ideas flowing up front. We will, of course, look at the challenges later. But we've found that once the negatives start, it makes it harder to do the creative thinking we need for the possible advantages. It's about the brain science of creativity."

Annika looked surprised and at a loss for words. Sally, good-naturedly, stated, "Annika, last week you mentioned to me that both of our firms have clientele the other could sell to. That is a great point to start with."

Annika seemed surprised again, as if she didn't expect to have her idea respected. Sally went on with greater energy now that everyone was paying attention, "Okay, everyone, we've all done our homework. Bring it on! What are other potential advantages?" Quickly, the brainstorm gained energy and ideas began to flow. Sally made sure to compliment Annika on the first few ideas she shared. Within ten minutes, Sally was pleased to notice that the lemon-eating expression was gone from Annika's face. She actually even smiled once after Jane mentioned Tiger's great sales records! They were well on their way to becoming a new, bigger and better firm.

Years later they were all able to laugh at how close they came to not merging successfully.

In this story, fearful Annika had been on track to unwittingly destroy the whole deal. Her Caveman was causing her to act from fight responses against others. Jane's caveman was putting her into a fight mode as well. Hiro started to ease the tension with humor. But even then, Sally had to focus them on their goals and give them a sense of a way through this conflict. If Sally hadn't been able to calm

Jane's Caveman, and then later Annika's, they would have left this meeting enraged at each other causing the deal to crumble. Once they were calmer, Sally was able to use a positive approach to creating solutions that energized everyone's Artists. This moved them from an "us vs. them" mentality to an inner movie of them all as a successful team.

Mastering Motivation: The Journey

Twenty-five hundred years ago, the Chinese philosopher Lao Tzu wisely stated, "A journey of a thousand miles begins with a single step." Mastery is the same way. It takes step after step in the right direction. I have my own model, which describes the journey of mastery a little more explicitly. Although we're going to measure this in hours, ten thousand of them, according to the research shared in Malcolm Gladwell's book *Outliers: The Story of Success*.

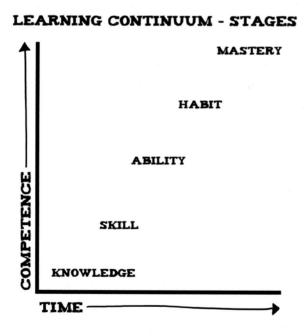

LEARNING CONTINUUM - STAGES

MASTERY

HABIT

ABILITY

SKILL

KNOWLEDGE

COMPETENCE

TIME

Read books to gain knowledge. Do the activities to earn skills.

Practice the skills successfully in many situations to develop the ability to use them where you want to. Perform these abilities long enough, and they will become habits you can do instinctively. And after ten thousand hours of practice, you will achieve mastery. That's when it becomes part of your personality.

When I was a teenager, people described me as shy, angry, depressed, and rebellious. Now people describe me as positive, outgoing, confident, and energizing. This transformation came from walking my journey of motivation mastery. I've seen thousands of my clients transform from being quite negative to becoming motivational. I've also seen hundreds of the trauma survivors I volunteer with become far more positive about themselves and their lives. You, too, will learn ways you can move yourself further along the continuum than you are today. Once you're far enough along, you'll create steps that specifically fit you. Part of how I've created my steps is borrowing from books, workshops and the masters themselves.

Energize yourself and those around you. Ignite passion and performance. Remember that sharing what you've learned will strengthen your skills. Most importantly, choose the life you want to lead! Whatever life brings to you, make the absolute best of it. Rewrite your inner autobiography to support you in reaching your dreams. Once you've reached your dreams, create new, inspiring dreams. You are the master of your life.

Stages of Mastering Motivation

Take the time to write your responses to the following. Your dreams are worth it!

These stages are designed to 1) Energize your Artist for your dreams 2) Calm your Caveman about the challenges of going after your dreams 3) Give your Thinker the tools it needs to help you create your dreams.

1. **Dream:** Create clear, compelling goals about what you want to accomplish, with greater motivation for your personal and work life.
   (Tip: Clear and compelling goals create an inner movie of you living your dream, and are written briefly so that you can remember them easily.)

2. **Build on strengths:** Make a list of at least twenty-five things you are already doing in your life that will help you towards these goals.
   (Tip: These strengths can be as wide-ranging as I "read this book," "got a degree in this area," "like using some of the skills I'll need to achieve my dream," "know people in that industry," "am very passionate about this," etc.)

3. **Build momentum:** Remind yourself of your top goals and the best things you're doing to accomplish those goals now.

4. **Learn new skills:** Circle the skills and ideas that are most likely to help you achieve your goals.

5. **Build momentum:** Regularly (at least weekly) remind yourself of your top goals and the best things you're already doing to accomplish those goals.

6. **Practice new skills:**
   a. List at least five situations where you can easily practice the skills you circled and improve them.
   b. Choose the best situation to practice the skills you

10:1 ratio positive:negative	Positive change reframes	Rewriting your inner autobiography	Positive change questions: Goals? What works? What else?
Chameleon effect	Positive priming	Motivational inner movies	Collecting 20 no's before giving up
Calming the Caveman	Energizing the Artist	Convincing the Thinker	Forming habits

selected. Begin. Learn from your experience. Improve. Repeat.

7. **Continue to build momentum:** Remind yourself of your top goals and the best things you're already doing to achieve those goals.

8. **Develop skills into abilities:**
   a. List at least twenty ideas for more challenging places you can practice these skills when you're ready.
   b. Choose one of these ideas and practice. Learn from it, improve, and practice again.

If you want more (free) ideas on how to use these tools, visit:

Action! Becoming a Master of Motivation

- The book's website, energizeperformance.com

- My firm's website, matchboxgroup.com/inspiring-tools

I love to hear how people are using these skills. Contact me with new ideas for igniting passion and performance by influencing inner movies and creating positive change.

Welcome to the positive change revolution.

Bob

Bob Faw

BIBLIOGRAPHY

Arneston, Amy, Carolyn Mazure, and Rajita Sinha. "This Is Your Brain in Meltdown." *Scientific American* (2012).

Bargh, J. A., M. Chen, and L. Burrows. "Automaticity of Social Behavior: Direct Effects of Trait Construct and Stereotype Priming on Action." *Journal of Personality and Social Psychology* 71 (1996): 230–244.

Beazley, Claire. "The Many Sides of Optimism." *Positive Psychology UK* (online journal, no date attributed).

Ben-Shahar, Tal David. Harvard Professor who teaches "Positive Psychology."

Blanchard, Kenneth and Spencer Johnson, MD. *The One Minute Manager.* New York: Berkley Books, 1982.

Blanchard, K., S. Fowler, and L. Hawkins. (2005) *Self Leadership and the One Minute Manager: Increasing Effectiveness through Situational Self Leadership.* CITY: Harper Collins Publishers, 2005.

Behncke, L. (2004) "Mental Skills Training For Sports: A Brief Review. Athletic Insight." *The Online Journal of Sports Psychology* 6, no. 1(March, 2004). http://www.athleticinsight.com/Vol6Iss1/ MentalSkillsReview.htm

Brafman, Rom and Ori Brafman. (2008) "Sway: The Irresistible Pull of Irrational Behavior."

Buckingham, Marcus, (2001) "Now, Discover Your Strengths"

Cameron, K.S. and A. Caza. "Developing Strategies for Responsible Leadership." In *Handbook on Responsible Leadership and Governance in Global Business,* eds. Jonathan P. Doh and Stephen Stumph. New York: Oxford University Press, 2005.

Chabris, Christopher and Daniel Simons. (2008) "The Invisible Gorilla: And Other Ways Our Intuitions Deceive Us."

Cooperrider, D.L. and S. Srivastva. "Appreciative Inquiry in Organizational Life." *Research in Organizational Change and Development* 1 (1987): 129–169.

Covey, Steven. *The Seven Habits of Highly Effective People*. Fireside, NY: Simon and Shuster Inc., 1989.

Csikszentmihalyi, Mihaly. *Beyond Boredom and Anxiety: Experiencing Flow in Work and Play*. San Francisco: Jossey-Bass, 1975.

Dijkshterhuis, Ap and Ad van Knippenberg. "The Relationship between Perception and Behavior, or How to Win a Game of Trivial Pursuit." *Journal of Personality and Social Psychology* 74, no. 4 (1998): 865–77.

Drucker, Peter. (1966) "The Effective Executive."

Eden, D. *Pygmalion in Management: Productivity as a Self-fulfilling Prophecy*. Lexington, MA: Lexington Books, 1990.

Eden, D., D. Geller, A. Gewirtz, R. Gordon-Terner, et al. "Implanting Pygmalion Leadership Style through Workshop Training: Seven Field Experiments." *Leadership Quarterly* 11(2000): 171–210.

Eden, D. "Self-fulfilling Prophecy as a Management Tool: Harnessing Pygmalion." *Academy of Management Review* 9 (1984): 64–73.

Eden, D. *Pygmalion in Management: Productivity as a Self-fulfilling Prophecy*. Lexington, MA: Lexington Books, 1990.

Eden, D. "Leadership and Expectations: Pygmalion Effects and Other Self-fulfilling Prophecies in Organizations." *Leadership Quarterly* 3 (1992): 271–305.

Faw, Bob. "An Old Sea Dog Can Learn New Tricks." *Seasonings*, Organizational Development Network online (2008). http://matchboxgroup.com/inspiring-tools

Faw, Bob. Bob Faw's Blog on creating positive change: bobfaw.wordpress.com.

Faw, Bob. "Staying Positive in Negative Times." *New Hampshire Business Review* (2009). http://matchboxgroup.com/inspiring-tools

Faw, Bob. "Improvisational Leadership: Greater Buy-in and Morale on the Fly." (2011) white paper. http://matchboxgroup.com/inspiring-tools.

Fredrick's Website: http://www.unc.edu/peplab/barb_fredrickson_page.html

Fredrickson, B. L. and M. Losada. "Positive Affect and the Complex Dynamics of Human Flourishing." *American Psychologist*, 60, no. 7 (2005): 678–686.

Gladwell, Malcolm. *Blink: The Power of Thinking without Thinking*. Boston: Little, Brown, 2005.

Goleman, Daniel. "Emotional Intelligence: Why It Can Matter More Than IQ" (2005).

Gottman, John and Sybil Carrere. "Predicting Divorce among Newlyweds from the First Three Minutes of a Marital Conflict Discussion." *Family Process* 38, no. 3 (1999): 293–301.

Hanson, Rick and Richard Mendius. "Buddha's Brain: The Practical Neuroscience of Happiness, Love, and Wisdom" (2009).

Kirschenbaum, D. S., A. M. Ordman, A. J. Tomarken, and R. Holtzbauer. "Effects of Differential Self-monitoring and Level of Mastery on Sports Performance: Brain Power Bowling." *Cognitive Therapy and Research* 6, no. 3 (1982): 335–42.

Jackson, Paul Z. and Mark McKergow. "The Solutions Focus."

Livingston, J. S. "Pygmalion in Management." *Harvard Business Review* 47, no. 4 (1969): 81–89.

Losada, M. and E. D. Heaphy. "The Role of Positivity and Connectivity in the Performance of Business Teams: A Nonlinear Dynamics Model." *American Behavioral Scientist* 47 (February 2004): 740–65.

Losada's Website: http://losada.socialpsychology.org/

McAndrew, Frank. "Can Gossip Be Good?" *Scientific American Mind* (October/November 2008).

Nicklaus, Jack. (2005) "Golf My Way."

Positive Deviance Method: positivedeviance.org

Rock, David and Jeffrey Schwartz. "Neuroscience of Leadership." *Strategy+Business* (2006).

Rosenthal, R. and L. Jacobson. *Pygmalion in the Classroom*. New York: Holt, Rinehart & Winston, 1968.

Rosenthal, Robert and Lenore Jacobson. "Pygmalion in the Classroom" Expanded edition. New York: Irvington, 1992.

Seligman, Martin. "Learned Optimism—How to Change Your Mind and Your Life" (2006).

Seligman, Martin. (1999) speech as President of American Psychological Association.

Sewell, D. F. "Attention-focusing Instructions and Training Times in Competitive Youth Swimmers." *Perceptual and Motor Skills* 83 (1996): 915–20.

Skosnik, P. D., R. T. Chatterton, Jr., T. Swisher, and S. Park. "Modulation of Attentional Inhibition by Norepinephrine and Cortisol after Psychological Stress." *International Journal of Psychophysiology* 36 (2000): 59–68.

Soothing the Amygdala: http://lifeatthebar.wordpress.com/2007/05/11 /anger-managing-the-amygdala-hijack

ACKNOWLEDGMENTS

In particular, I'd like to give thanks to:

All the people I've worked with over the years. I think that I've learned more from you all than I've taught you. That humbles me. Thank you all for sharing with me what works for you, and helping me know what ideas to keep sharing, which to adapt, and which to dropkick.

My sweetheart, Zsuzsi Gero. Zsuzsi, you've stood by me through thick and thin throughout this process. You supported me when neck injuries and Lyme Disease almost made me give up. Your love and enthusiasm have kept me going. You've also been really helpful with your feedback on my many drafts, and your brilliant flashes of insight have been priceless.

My editor, Stacy Ennis. Stacy, your great insights helped me turn my spoken word into something that makes sense in the written word. This was much harder than I ever would have imagined, and I couldn't have done it without you. You were also my muse, inspiring me to create new concepts to better explain my ideas. You are fantastic! Any writer is lucky to have you on his/her side. (The fact that you worked so hard right up to your due date made me feel like we were both expectant mothers).

My publisher, Maryanna Young at Aloha Publishing. You are a master at energizing me, especially at times when my "inner movie" imagined dead ends in the writing process. I never realized a publisher could be a true partner in helping me create a book, and you're helping me improve my speaking career as well. You are a true partner.

My business partner, Michael McCann. Your nonstop creativity has helped me enhance every aspect of my work. I appreciate your pushing me to improve everything, all the time. Also, your positive feedback and cheering have helped me gain the confidence for the intimidating venture of writing a book.

There are so many dear friends who have been "colleagues in transformation". Thank you Eric and Karen Lautzenheiser, Annette Martens, Rick and Sara Martel, Rick Davis, Debbie Korn, Tricia Flynn, and so many others.

I'm also very grateful to all of those who have written and spoken so eloquently about motivation. Thank you, greats of motivation such as Dale Carnegie, Zig Ziglar, Tony Robbins, Nick Vujicic, Winston Churchill, Aristotle, the Brafman brothers, the Heath brothers, Bart Simpson, and so many more.

I'm also in grateful awe of the amazing neuroscientists who have provided so many wonderful insights into what makes our brains tick. Thank you to you brainiacs such as John Medina, Dov Eden, John Gottman, Vilayanur Ramachandran, Sam Harris, etc.

Lastly, but equally important, I want to thank all of you who change your lives against the odds. And, I'm so grateful for those who energize others to rise beyond their horizons to achieve new heights as yet undreamed.

ABOUT THE AUTHOR

Bob Faw is a positive change consultant, transformational thought leader, and sought after dynamic speaker who motivates people around the world to make positive changes in their lives. A trusted consultant to organizations like Harvard Business School, Merck, American Red Cross, American Cancer Society and Applebee's, Bob works with companies to set a foundation for positive change with lasting performance. His strategic insights and improvisational comedic approach help people embrace new ideas, energize vision and objectives, and make continuing transformations in their lives and organizations.

In his paid and volunteer work, he's seen the best and worst of people and has emerged a practical optimist who loves people more all the time. He also co-founded and volunteers with the nonprofit Vital Cycles, helping people transform their lives.

Bob lives in New Hampshire with Zsuzsi Gero (his sweetheart) and Nisha (his dog). His passions include hiking, dancing, swimming and learning from brain science.

For more information, visit www.energizeperformance.com.